For the Love of
Frenchies

For the Love of
Frenchies

The Dogs That Changed My Life

Pete Wicks

Foreword by **Marc Abraham**

1 3 5 7 9 10 8 6 4 2

Virgin Books, an imprint of Ebury Publishing,
20 Vauxhall Bridge Road,
London SW1V 2SA

Virgin Books is part of the Penguin Random House group of
companies whose addresses can be found at
global.penguinrandomhouse.com

Penguin
Random House
UK

First published in the United Kingdom by Virgin Books in 2018

www.penguin.co.uk

A CIP catalogue record for this book is available from
the British Library

ISBN 9780753548998

All photos courtesy of Pete Wicks, apart from page 7 bottom
image, and page 8 bottom image © James Rudland

Designed and typeset by K.DESIGN, Winscombe, Somerset
Printed and bound in Great Britain by Clays Ltd, St Ives PLC

Penguin Random House is committed to a sustainable future
for our business, our readers and our planet. This book is made
from Forest Stewardship Council® certified paper.

For Ernest ...   you were not just a dog, not just a pet and not just my best friend, you were my family. Not a day goes by that I'm not thankful for the time I spent with you and thankful for the lessons you taught me. Eric misses his brother and I miss the leader of my Wolfpack. You made me a better man. Forever in my heart.

Contents

Foreword by

Marc Abraham
BVM&S MRCVS

AS A PRACTICING veterinary surgeon I meet a lot of people and a lot of pets. My job is my passion and everything I do is, in some way, connected to the job of caring for animals – and that usually includes the people associated with them too. Being a vet is not a career path you can follow if you don't truly care about the amazing pets you meet and treat every day, and of course you have to be there for the owners to help them do their best; resulting in happy, healthy pets all round.

As well as working in a small vet practice in Peacehaven near Brighton, I also do media work, which brings an added responsibility to my vocation. It gives me a platform and a voice to speak out for the animals – the voiceless – and to help try and educate the masses as well as influence positive change. I'm a great believer in using the tools we have to help those more vulnerable than us, so when Pete Wicks approached me to write this foreword for this book, I was both honoured and excited.

One of the first times I met Pete, we were at an animal welfare event at the House of Commons. I was there as a guest of the charity Humane Society International (HSI), who were hosting a reception to highlight the horrific dog meat trade in South Korea. I was interested to know why Pete had chosen to be there, and didn't have to wait long to discover that he is deadly serious about both his passion for dogs and the global issues of dog welfare in general.

It's not often that you meet a television personality who is as committed to his beliefs as Pete Wicks. This guy doesn't just 'like' dogs; he is a full-on 'dog man', especially when it comes to his two French bulldogs Ernest and Eric. French bulldogs are a huge part of his life (as one glance at his Instagram page will show), but there is a dark side to this love story.

It's no surprise to pet-lovers that pet loss can be both serious and debilitating. Perhaps not an issue that someone who's never had a pet would take seriously, but pet bereavement is responsible for lost time at work, as well as mental health issues including loneliness, a killer in its own right. Pets really do mean *everything* to some people. And Pete knows this better than most, after suddenly and shockingly losing his adored Frenchie Ernest in 2016.

And it's not just Ernest. The whole French bulldog breed is in trouble: although it is on track to topple traditional pedigree dogs like the Labrador in the popularity stakes, it's tragically at a cost to the breed's health and welfare. And in my opinion, this usually stems from intensive, irresponsible breeding and selling. Battery-farmed dogs are forced to breed on every heat with no vet care, no proper diet, and not even a clean or caring environment to raise their puppies. Puppy farming is about one thing only: money. Current legislation allows these pups to be sold to unsuspecting owners via the legal third-party market, so in 2009 I launched Pup Aid, a national campaign to close these avenues that enable those greedy and uncaring puppy farmers to reach their unsuspecting customers. This will result in accountable breeders, transparency in the market, and most importantly, dogs will become happier and healthier.

Sadly, Frenchies are just one of the pedigree breeds hit by this trade which occurs both legally and illegally, with other fashionable breeds like pugs and dachshunds amongst others, suffering greatly too. Many of these cute and adorable breeds are susceptible to serious health issues and an unhappy life, even once they escape the puppy farms. Not to mention their mums left behind. Surely we owe these poor dogs more?

Pete's knowledge of the health and welfare problems facing his favourite breed, the French bulldog, is impressive and he's always striving to learn more. And even better he wants to DO more. These dogs are suffering not just because of cruel individuals, but because so many key influencers and lawmakers appear reluctant to confront, acknowledge or deal with these problems efficiently. It takes strong voices to speak out and create change, and Pete is someone who I know will keep the faith for Frenchies and for all dogs.

With a colossal social media following of over 1 million people, Pete is able to harness people power – the power of the mob – to spread messages of awareness far and wide to a loyal fanbase, who can in turn follow his passion, his lead, and we can all work together to help improve the lives of dogs.

I see health problems associated with irresponsible breeding in my surgery day-in day-out, and with current legislation allowing – and even encouraging – pups to be sold without their mums away from where they were born (an almost sure sign of puppy farming), the problems aren't going to go away until these laws change. There also needs to be increased public awareness of the correct way to choose a dog, and in this book, Pete gives important advice, including recommendations to always see a pup interacting with its mum in the place he or she was born, or better still to rescue a dog in need. These lessons have never been so important, or so timely.

Pete has personally experienced the need for dogs' lives to be improved. He's opened many a door into shocking and saddening situations and experiences for dogs, but most importantly, he didn't shut them again and walk away like so many. Pete stepped through and discovered what he can do to help – and I'm proud to know and work alongside him to make sure positive change happens.

Pete's incredible dog welfare work and support of my Pup Aid campaign means we move a step closer to ending puppy farming, irresponsible breeding, and encouraging rescue pet adoption. Will you join us?

Marc Abraham BVM&S MRCVS

The Geezer in the Fur Coat

24 August 2016

Words cannot describe how heartbroken I am to have suddenly lost one of the best things to have ever come into my life. My boy Ernest wasn't just a dog to me, he was my best friend. Things will never be the same.

I am thankful to him for teaching me a lot about myself and everything about unconditional love. He will always be in my heart. R.I.P.

Ernest#Wolfpack

MY DOG ERNEST was a geezer. He was a bloke's bloke. Know what I mean? If he had been born human, we would have enjoyed a pint and some chat down the local where he'd laugh and crack jokes in rasping Ray Winstonesque tones. Ern was always the life and soul of the party, happy to be at my side, nudging into my chest and smiling: 'All right, my son?'

To me, Ern was a proper East Ender. And like his namesake, my Uncle Ernest, a good old boy, a generous salt-of-the-earth character to the core. Ern may have had a fur coat and four legs, but he was the kind of creature I knew that I could trust, who would patiently hear me out and know how to keep a secret. I trusted him. I loved him. And he loved me back.

When I rescued Ern's adopted brother, Eric, it was the happiest time. Those two Frenchies were the centre of my universe. We were the 'Wolfpack', an invincible team: me as pack leader, Ern as our tough-guy body-guard and Eric as our loveable joker. We went every-where together, and life was sweet in a way I hadn't thought possible.

For a while I felt I had it all: success in business, the Wolfpack and my exciting new venture into television with ITVBe's *TOWIE* (*The Only Way Is Essex*). I guessed that this was how happy was supposed to feel. I certainly hadn't known it before. But on Wednesday 24 August 2016, my happy world came to a shocking, agonising standstill.

Ern died and so did a part of me.

If I could have that day over again I'm sure I would do things differently. Or at least that's what I have told myself a million times over. Every time I replay those moments in my head I tell myself that I failed. That I could have done more for Ern. The funny thing is, if it had been raining we wouldn't have left the house at all.

Ernest hated the rain. I can see him now, standing at the door of our ground-floor apartment, his lumpy front paws planted firmly indoors, his face screwed up at the sight of raindrops. On days like that he would turn his silky, fawn-coloured head towards me, his eyes saying: 'Dad, are you serious? You can't want me to go out in this? Really?'

I only had one answer for him. 'Yes mate, I'm very serious; now let's get going.' I always thought I was in charge, but who was I kidding? I think we both knew that Ern always called the shots. As for walking in the rain … the first puddle we hit – dead standstill. And when Ern decided he didn't want to do anything, he absolutely didn't do it. If I was stupid enough to make him go out, I'd end up jumping the puddles like an overgrown toddler and holding Ern in my arms!

It seemed such a pain back then but now I'd give anything to carry him through the rain with Eric plodding at my heels. It was funny, and all the time Ern gave me his 'grateful look' – that's the one where the corner of his mouth turned up and his big, dark eyes smiled. He knew he had me, every time.

There was no rain that day in August 2016. It wasn't a hot day, but it was warm and breezy, so I had plenty of water for Ern and Eric and they looked happy to be out in the fresh air. Ern had given the day his usual double-nose-take on the doorstep before deciding to make a move, which was good enough to encourage Eric to follow him. The boys blinked in the sunshine, I donned my shades and the Wolfpack headed for the park.

I was in a good mood and it was one of those great days that calls to you to get outdoors – you know what I mean? And I'm lucky to have plenty of places locally to go for walks and plenty more just a short drive away.

That day it was enough to go to the park where the dogs could bustle along at their own pace and I could trail behind them, lead in hand.

There's me, such a proud dad, watching Ern stomping along at tough geezer pace ... Eric, his solid body rocking in Ern's shadow. I loved that. That was us – me, Ern and Eric out on a walk on a beautiful Essex summer's day.

Eric, bless him, always wants to be friends with everyone and still has to learn the hard way that most dogs respect personal space and few dogs appreciate his rush to sniff their bum. If Ern was Ray Winstone then Eric has to be Alan Carr ... right in the face and givin' it a bit of chat here and there without taking a breath. That day Eric was on top form being super-chatty, which left Ern doing his protective big brother act and me in dad mode. We both let our guy waddle ahead while we stayed at a safe distance ready to step in if another dog decided to turn on him. Pity, that happens too often. If he was a human Eric would be the kind of mate you would love for his easy company and – let's be honest – daftness, but at the same time you'd want to protect him from himself.

Eric, I love ya but sometimes you're such a doughnut!

As it turned out we didn't stay out too long that day. After about an hour I could see that Ern was starting to pant a bit heavier than normal. It was time to go home.

When we stepped in through the front door Ern went straight to his drinking bowl and then flopped out on the wooden floor in the hall, just as he always did. It wasn't long before I could hear him snoring. Good old proper snoring it was too. I decided that I'd take a leaf out of Ern's book and crashed out on the bed.

I woke about an hour later with Eric pawing at my face.

When I came around all I could hear was Ern breathing but he wasn't in his usual place lying on my bed. I leapt through to the hall, but he had moved from there. Something was wrong. I stood still for a second to tune into the low, hollow, rasping noise, which led me straight to the spot where Ern was lying on the cold tiles of the bathroom floor. Eric was standing over him wearing an expression that said: 'What's wrong, Dad? Help him.'

What the f**k?! I grabbed every towel I could lay my hands on, threw them into the bath and turned the cold tap on. Then I lay the cool, soaked towels over Ern's body and called the vet.

The next few minutes are still a blur, but I must have managed to lift Ern and the heap of soggy towels into the back of the car and I know that Eric was with me because he would never have left Ern. All I could hear was Ern's shallow breathing and Eric's high-pitched whimpering. Horrible noises. I can still recall them. The whimpering was worse. It kind of drills into your head, but I couldn't leave Eric at home, he was far too stressed. I lifted him into the car and we set off the couple of miles to the vet's surgery.

My head was somewhere else – or at least I wished it was. I don't know how fast I was going but the police didn't catch up with me. Funny how even the shortest journey can seem like the longest when you know that everything rests on your actions.

I can't remember arriving at the surgery or parking or being shown into the consulting room. 'It's a heart attack,' the vet's words rang in my head. 'I'm sorry but all we can do right now is apply ice to cool Ernest down, watch over him and hope for the best. I promise you we'll do all we can for him here. I promise you that.'

I couldn't have asked for more, but I thought, if I believed in God, now was the time to pray. Eric was with me the whole time and he was not in great shape. I know it sounds awful, but all my focus was on Ern – but then I could tell that Eric's focus was on Ern too.

I watched over him. Didn't take my eyes off him.

'How's he doing?', I asked the vet. I needed to know.

'Well, I think we're on the right side of it now, Pete, but let's not count our chickens quite yet. We'll keep him on obs, won't let him out of our sight and just go where Ernest takes us.'

I could feel the edge of panic slip away as if someone had pressed an emotional dimmer switch. I knew Ern wasn't out of the woods, but he looked as if he was coming around. I needed to let my mum know what was going on and this seemed to be my chance for a quick call.

I cried my way through every word as I explained the whole thing to Mum. 'Pete, it sounds like you did all you could. Even the vet said you did all you could for Ernest so please don't blame yourself,' she said. Listening to Mum I could tell that she had obviously guessed how guilty I felt but as I was responsible for his care it was difficult for me to see it any other way. 'How's Ernest now, sweetheart? When can you bring him home?'

I didn't know the answer to that and I didn't want to stay any longer on the phone. 'Gotta go and check, Mum. I'll let you know.'

I headed back into the consulting room with poor Eric at my heels and there, right in front of me, was a scene I hadn't prepared for. I never dream. I just don't and never have, but this was a nightmare for sure. The vet and her team were standing over Ern. Their faces said it all: NO! NO! Oh my God, NO!

Ern had flatlined on the table. My boy Ernest was gone. The tears arrived and wouldn't stop. I hated the tears and the reason for them. I was hurting. It just hurt like hell.

Eric was in a state, shaking and whimpering. He had seen more than me because the little man had been with Ern in the bathroom before coming to wake me. And now I was no use to him. My head was in a right mess. It was blown. I couldn't believe what was going on. Somebody needed to wake me up because surely this couldn't be happening?

The wonderful vet and her team were very understanding and said I could stay in the consulting room with Ern for as long as I liked. I probably stayed longer than they expected but I didn't want to leave my boy. I tickled Ern's lovely, wrinkly, still-warm belly just as I always did but this time there was no reaction. He was so still and that wasn't right. He had this spot where, if you tickled him, one leg would automatically kick like crazy. It was always so funny. But not that day. I spoke to him; I asked if he blamed me. I asked if he could forgive me.

I sobbed so hard I thought my chest would burst.

Somehow, I found myself in the car, heading for home. Eric refused to go in the back, so I had to secure him in the front seat, but he was shaking so much it scared me a little bit because I didn't know what to do to help him. Our return journey was long and silent except for the loud thumping in my head – I'd failed to bring Ern home and I dreaded walking back through the front door without him.

I called my mum who had been waiting to hear that we were home so that she could come over. I was trying to hold back so that my distress didn't add to Eric's upset but as soon as I saw Mum I collapsed into her arms and, although I was twenty-seven years old at the time, I cried like a little boy. I've never shown emotion easily, Mum knows that, but I'd never experienced loss like this before. She held me and cuddled Eric at the same time.

It was good to have such closeness but suddenly I had an overwhelming urge to get out of the flat. Mum understood that I needed to be on my own to try to work out how to cope with what had happened. I rushed out towards the park for some space where I could shout, scream and punch a few trees. I shouted until I was hoarse and lashed out until my knuckles were bleeding but, as I walked back home, I knew it wasn't enough.

And Eric?

In hindsight, I'm not sure I did the right thing but at the time I thought he would be better off spending time with my nan. To be honest I came to the conclusion that it would be better for both of us: Nan loves Eric and she would give him plenty of cuddles and know what to do. I didn't know anything and felt I would be better off on my own for a few days.

As soon as I got back from dropping off Eric I went straight to the bathroom and fell on the floor. The tears returned and did not stop.

I slept on the bathroom floor for three days. Then I brought Eric home and we slept side by side on the bathroom floor, every night for two weeks. Eric wouldn't leave, and I didn't want to see anyone. So, we did nothing – together.

Sleeping in the place where we last saw Ern alive was comforting.

Now we only had each other, and I was well aware that Eric was giving me more support than I was capable of giving to him. After a few days I found enough strength to take him for a walk over the field but almost as soon as I stepped outdoors I broke down in a heap of tears, shouting at myself: 'I'm a terrible dad! I shouldn't have taken Ern out that day. I should have made sure he had more rests or at least I should have seen some warning signs. Why didn't I see them?'

I have a small, close family, so it was lovely that over the days that followed Ern's death they folded in around me to protect me, but I was in a weird cycle of wanting comfort and then struggling to break free. No matter how hard anyone tried they couldn't say anything that could help me – or Eric. We were in our own little bubble of grief and I couldn't explain how painful it was for us. So it was easier to send people away than try to bare my feelings. I appreciate that probably doesn't make sense but that's how it was.

And then there was social media, which at any other time is a total blessing but at that moment in my life was a curse. It was six days before I felt capable of sharing my dreadful news with my followers on Twitter and Facebook. My family and my mates told me that I would feel better and that it would help me come to terms with Ern's passing, but I really wasn't ready. I know everyone meant well and they were doing their best to comfort me, but I just wasn't in a place to cope with these new feelings. I probably behaved very badly and I'm sorry for that. Ern had gone, and I was lost, angry and wanted to hide away.

Hiding was fine for me – but what about Eric?

Eric was in a really deep, blue funk, missing his big brother. If there was one time I wished he could talk to me it was then. The dynamics of our little family had changed: the Wolfpack was a 'wolf' down and the gap in our lives was suddenly huge.

To make it worse there were the reminders of how things used to be for us as a team.

The week after we lost Ern it had to be business as usual for the photoshoot for my 2017 calendar but it was not normal in any way because Ern wasn't with us. Eric stepped up to the mark and did his bit, bless him, but he wasn't comfortable posing for the camera, he never is – that was Ern's speciality. Ern loved the camera and it loved him. Things that had been fun with Ern around were now just routine; we were just going through the motions of getting up, going to work and going to sleep. We were just getting things done.

I hated this stage of missing Ern. Mostly because it wasn't fair on Eric and the more we did without Ernest made me more aware of the horrific responsibility I had for Eric. The problem was, everything I tried to do for him felt wrong or not good enough. I couldn't bring Ern back and I knew that was the only thing that would take Eric's pain away.

And that wasn't all. I was convinced that Eric blamed me for Ern leaving us. I felt he was picking up on my negativity, which was making everything worse – it was all because of me and my shortcomings as his dad. And that's the nub of it – I felt guilty. I hated myself for it and I felt I deserved to be punished in some way.

I guess I was in shock. If Ern had been ill, then I would have had time to prepare and come to terms with knowing that his ill health would take him. But everything was normal ... it had been a normal day, walking the dogs, and then my world had suddenly ended. In my book that's not fair. That's not how it was supposed to be. We were the Wolfpack – indestructible.

Without Ern, Eric and I were flung into a very dark place. And I wasn't sure how we were going to get out of it. While I was in the middle of the whirl of guilt, anger, confusion, shut-out and shut-down I failed to appreciate the massive positive that Eric was still alive and wonderful: yes, we had lost Ray Winstone, but we still had Alan Carr and he really is a funny little f**ker!

When I said Eric's name he looked at me and I saw that he was trying to carry on as normal – for me. Truth is, for 364 days of 2016 we had good times, me and Eric. It was time to count my blessings and the inspiration for getting up and dusting myself down was right there in front of me in a blue-fawn coat.

Eric was and is the joker in the Wolfpack: the loveable doughnut. And who doesn't love a doughnut? Eric needed me and there was only one thing for it: I needed to man up and STEP UP – for him.

Without Ern, it was all up to me and I have never felt

so alone and angry. Looking back, I think it was pure emotional overload that made me react this way but even as I write this I can still recall the whirling feelings of loss, loneliness and panic that were compressing my chest. It's not easy to function with a chunk of emotional concrete weighing you down but I now realise that's all part of the normal grieving process. Surviving it, stage by stage, I gradually came to see that all we both needed to do was learn how to live differently – without Ern.

I held on to the thing that Ern had given to me and then Ern and Eric had given me together – loyal companionship. The Wolfpack is the most honest relationship I have ever known and probably will ever know. But that's because dogs only do honest. They're only capable of unconditional love and don't make the human mistake of promising more than they can deliver when it comes to emotional honesty. I still had all of that with Eric. Ern didn't take that with him.

Ern taught me a lot about myself when he was alive, and his loss is still teaching me more every day. I didn't lose him because I was a rubbish dad but, just like it said in my school reports, I could have done better. In my mind if I use the grief to learn more now I can do better for Eric and through that journey repay my debt to my mate, Ern.

That's Ern's legacy: it's time to learn what I'm made of and what I can give back to the Frenchies who adopted me, gave so much to me and made me a less selfish human being just by knowing them.

Chapter 1

The Wolfpack

Becoming a dad to Ern and Eric

BEING A DAD to Ern and then to Eric has, without a shadow of a doubt, changed my life. So much so that I find myself thinking of my life as having three stages: Life Before Ern, Life With Ern and now Life After Ern.

Sometimes I really have to think what it was like before I owned a dog because being a member of our homemade Wolfpack became the greatest and the best part of being me. Although, to be honest – and I will be honest with you – I can now see that acquiring Ernest was entirely selfish.

You know what? If I had considered dog ownership the way responsible people do I think I would have declared myself totally unsuitable at that time in my life. Why? Because I was floating. My nan will tell you that I didn't have my feet on the ground; I was a party boy who didn't take anything seriously, especially myself. She called me a 'Lost Soul' which, thinking back, was a bit upsetting, but only because she was right. I have the words LOST SOUL tattooed on my fingers now. Maybe to remind myself not to go there again because it's not a great place to be.

I knew that I needed an anchor in my life and then, one day, I saw a French bulldog being walked along the street, a cute little blue-fawn. I made my mind up right there and then that I wanted one.

What a little geezer! What a perfect little 'man dog'. That squidgy, smiley face, huge eyes, crazy bat ears, stocky body, solid little legs, 'square' head and a chest like a full-on bullfrog. What wasn't there to like about a Frenchie? So, I did what I always do when I have a purchase in mind – I went shopping.

I looked online and saw that they came in different colours, identified a few breeders and started to shop around. I decided I liked the red-fawn colouring and it had to be a boy-dog. It was just my preference and a bit of a silly macho thing but that's how it was so ... I went to see a couple of litters just to see what was on offer. They say that dogs choose us and, whether you believe that or not, it's true that Ern chose me.

When I went to see the litter of four puppies he was the one who headed for me. He played with my shoelaces and danced about; his little, gangly, ginger legs all over the place, big black eyes right in my face trying to attract my attention. He didn't need to do all of that: I was watching him the whole time. The breeder noticed that too. 'Oh, I'm so sorry, that one's already spoken for,' she said, as I wrapped my hand around the pup's tiny, shiny little body and he licked it happily in return.

Hers were not the words I wanted to hear. I was offered one of the other pups in the litter, but I was way past being tempted. I had already met the one I wanted to take home.

I was so disappointed. Funny how you're not too bothered about something until someone tells you that you can't have it. Then it eats at you. Right? Well, that's how it was with Ern. I became obsessed. I really wanted that little guy. He had my name all over him.

You can imagine my reaction when that same breeder called me a couple of weeks later to say that Ern's prospective owners decided they weren't able to take him after all. He was mine if I still wanted him. Lady Luck was on my side. Did I want him? Do me a favour – he was all I wanted.

Now, I wouldn't want to call Ern the biggest impulse buy in my collection but I said 'yes' to buying him quicker than I've ever said 'yes' to a new car, a flash suit or a pair of Italian shoes. I've probably spent longer choosing a new tattoo.

Ern was ten weeks old when he came home with me, and when the breeder handed him over I felt close to how I imagine it must feel when the midwife hands you your baby to hold for the first time. My heart was racing, my head buzzing. My face ached with smiling from ear to ear. I was as happy as Larry.

As I drove away from the breeder's house with Ern secured in his little basket I knew my life would never be the same again. There he was, this little geezer totally dependent on me for his every need. He had those great big black eyes on me and I hoped he sensed that I was up to the job. He was good in the car and I was happy with that because I didn't intend to do much without him. I was keen to show him off to my family and friends and, the way I looked at it, he would be going everywhere with me. As I drove along I imagined us going to all kinds of places together where we could hang out and chill out, guys together. Sweet.

When we got home I took the dog basket inside and gently set it down on the hall floor. So, this was it. Just the two of us. What do I do now?

I wasn't sure, but I thought I'd start by introducing my new pint-sized mate to his new surroundings. As I lifted him out of the basket he shivered a little and I guessed that was a small attack of nerves as he took in the rush of new sights and smells. At first his little feet slipped a little on the wooden floor, but he soon got the hang of it and managed a slow plod into the living room where the huge, L-shaped sofa must have looked as big as a New York skyscraper to a toddler. He tried to follow the line of it but all the looking up forced his glossy red rear-end down onto the rug. Then his head came down, his already bat-like ears stood up and he tilted his head right then left as his big round eyes settled on me. I smiled, and he licked his lips right up to his flat, black nose.

He sat there for a few seconds, only his eyes moving up, down and around and I wondered if he was thinking how quiet it was without his brothers and sisters. I assumed he would be feeling a bit lonely and maybe a bit scared, so I decided I'd fill the silence with a bit of chat telling him all about me and what a great time we were going to have together. He didn't move. Maybe because he was trying to work me out. Maybe it was my long hair, or the beard or both plus the noise of me gabbing away and striding around. I must have looked like a giant, clockwork, wind-up toy. He couldn't take his eyes off me.

I picked him up and took him into the kitchen to show him his food and water bowls and then back into the living room to show him his bed, on the floor just beyond the sofa, which was strewn with dog toys. I picked up each toy in turn, squeezed, shook and dangled them for his entertainment. He didn't seem impressed.

Food. That's it, always a good move when getting to know someone. I gave him a small helping of the brand that the breeder had recommended and he guzzled it down, no trouble. That's my boy! Loves his food – just like his dad. This was going well.

I was smitten. This little guy had stolen my heart.

'Life With Ern' had begun.

Twenty-four hours into dog ownership and I'm wondering – what the hell is going on? The adorable bundle of silky fun that I had picked up from the breeder the previous day was now busily chewing everything in sight and pissing on anything he didn't chew. Monster. This wasn't in any of the books – was it? I didn't know because I hadn't read any of them. I hadn't asked anyone what to expect either. Although I'm pretty sure this wasn't what I had signed up for.

My family had a dog when I was a child – Arnie. He was a rescue German shepherd: a lot of hair and teeth but friendly and he was my mate. He would lie on my bed, curl up next to me to watch television, eat the treats I smuggled for him and he always sensed when I needed him around for company and a hug. Arnie was the family dog but, to me, he was fun and my friend. I could enjoy every second of our time together without having to do the feeding, grooming and general cleaning up after him.

I didn't have anything to do with Arnie's puppy training. I would have remembered that bit, for sure.

I was just a kid back then enjoying the fun side of having a puppy in the house, so I guess the practical, non-fluffy stuff fell to my mum, who did what mums do and just cleaned everything up, like magic. I didn't see a thing. If I had I would have had a better idea of what having a dog really involved. As it was, when I felt that something was missing in my mid-twenties, it was the warm and fuzzy feelings of my bond with Arnie that I harked back to. Maybe, subconsciously, I was reaching for that feeling again and I think that the day I saw the stranger's little Frenchie in the street something clicked. Suddenly, there was the answer to what I thought I was searching for and I found it when I brought home Ern. But not for a second did I imagine him chewing my sofa.

All I knew at the time was that this pukka little geezer looked good and would accessorise my life perfectly. Back then, I wasn't thinking about how I could enhance his life. After all, it was still all about me.

Although he had only shown how good he was at chewing furniture and destroying expensive rugs, my new mate had also managed to muster enough puppy energy to read my insecurity to perfection – from his first night, he slept on my bed and high up on my chest.

For the first few days my new puppy was simply called ... 'Puppy'. It suited him, and he answered to it, but I could tell that he wasn't totally happy about it. I wondered if he thought I was a bit lazy and couldn't be bothered to come up with something more inspired. It wasn't that, it's just that I needed to get to know the little guy before landing him with a name for life. Ern had a wisdom all his own and I noticed it the first time I saw him with the rest of his litter. He had personality and he had great eyebrows: not the hairy kind – Frenchies don't have those – but a set of lovely little creases above his big, dark eyes.

When he wasn't happy he looked like a little old man with a furrowed, wrinkly brow. The little creases deepened and gathered between his eyes, his flat, black nose seemed to sit higher, almost meeting his brows, and his giant bat ears reached for the sky. If his mouth didn't always look as if it was going to break into a full 'joker' smile he would have got away with such a serious expression, but it never lasted long. The next second his eyes dropped, he was quickly stamping his front paws, one up and one down, his pink tongue lolled out and he looked like he was just about to tell you the best joke you've ever heard.

And when he did that ... he bore an uncanny resemblance to my Uncle Ernest.

Ernest? Now that was a good name. A proper East End name and it really suited him. There was only one potential problem: how would my nan feel about me calling my dog after her late brother?

If there was one person I would never want to upset, it's my nan. I would go so far as to say that she is more my best mate than my mum's mum. When people hear us speak to each other they are often shocked because we never do anything like typical grandmother and grandson 'chat'. We never have done. We are very close and very rude to each other! We call each other some crude names but it's all in affection and I love her to pieces.

It all goes back to when I was very young and a bit of a naughty boy to boot. I'd go out to play but always manage to end up at my nan's where she would let me mess about, spread my toys out and generally get away with murder. She never minded and was always pleased to see me and to spend time talking and laughing with me. When I became an angry young man, Nan was there for me again. She could always calm me down and help me to make sense of things. She didn't have an answer for everything, but she knew me well enough to get through my thick, shaven skull with a few words that would make me see the error of my ways. My nan is a very special lady who still lets me be me.

You know I love my nan to pieces, and she loves me to the moon and back, which is why her opinion on my dog's name really mattered. Nan would have the final word. No idea why I worried, though, because Nan loved the idea. She loved her brother Ernest and as soon as she met my Ern she loved him too. That was it then – Ernest had arrived!

When I made an appointment at the local vet's surgery to register Ernest I didn't think it was anything more than putting his name down and that would be it. He was a puppy and a healthy little guy, so I didn't expect to be visiting the surgery any time soon. Registering and the initial consultation was, in my mind, just a formality.

Don't get me wrong, I was listening to the vet and I heard him say that French bulldogs were fast becoming the most popular breed of dog in the UK. Back in 2013 they were hot on the heels of the Labrador and the lovely pug and I wasn't surprised that everyone wanted to get their hands on a Frenchie; after all, they are so bloody cute. Ernest looked happy being examined, everything was going OK and I was buzzing every time my little man-dog looked to me for reassurance as a child would to their dad.

As the vet was chatting about the breed, telling me about some of the health concerns and asking how I had acquired Ern I didn't think any of what he was saying applied to me. Yes, he'd had all the necessary vaccinations and I knew what was still needed and when … I had all of that in my head. I had it all covered, and I just wanted to go buy my boy some flash equipment and lots of toys. I'd seen some designer collars and leads, all that kind of thing, which would suit Ern perfectly. The vet talked about some of the potential heart and breathing problems with the breed but, to be honest, it went in one ear and out the other.

The vet also asked me how I was getting on with Ern's toilet training and I was proud to say that all was now going well – after some initial teething, weeing and trashing problems. As for formal training and behaviour classes I had all the contact numbers but we seemed to be muddling through the other stuff together. Getting it wrong some of the time and then getting it right the rest. We were OK. It was sweet.

It was the next step that gave me my first inkling that owning a dog was probably not going to be all about me after all. It was lovely to have Ern sleeping on my chest at night, being my adoring shadow and my boy but the big practical side of things had to be sorted out too, including me going to work, acquiring consultants for the NHS. There was only one thing for it – I would take him with me.

It was a great idea – at first – because it was so easy. I took the train into the city every day and Ern just loved it. He sat still on my lap or lay on my feet and behaved like the perfect gentleman with everyone around him. At the firm's offices in St Katharine Docks, close to the Tower of London, Ernest became a celebrity in his own right. He would potter around saying hello to everyone, begging any treats that were going. The girls thought he was the best thing ever to happen in the workplace and I got used to hearing comments like: 'Oh, he's so lovely …' as we walked by, and I knew they were talking about Ern, not me!

The other guys didn't mind Ern being around either although they knew my dog was the perfect babe magnet. In their words: 'Mate, you must get all the birds with that dog!' Truth is, Ern got their attention for himself. As I said, he was always the better part of me. He was also a major celebrity in his own Essex and City circles way before we joined *The Only Way Is Essex* and he dealt with all the attention like a true professional. He just loved it and he loved being with me. But that was the problem.

My work was based in London but I often had to travel overseas, and it was this aspect of the job that made me realise I needed a back-up plan for Ernest whenever I was called away on business. There was only one thing for it:

I needed a dog-sitter. And in my mind, there was only one person for the job – if she would take it.

'Nan, will you look after Ern while I'm at work?' Her first answer was, I'll be honest, unprintable! But, as it turned out, it was Ern who worked his magic that day. Ern was with me when I asked Nan the million-dollar question and it was as if he knew exactly what he needed to do to get the answer his dad wanted and needed to hear. He was all over her! He played all the puppy tricks, just as he did with me when I first saw him with the others in his litter. He was the bright spark that day and here he was turning on the charm for my nan. She couldn't resist him. He captured her heart as he had done mine and that's how she came to spend so much time with Ern and love him, as she said, like another grandson.

'He's such a naughty boy!' Nan used to say about Ern. 'He reminds me of you, Pete, when you were little!' Yes, thanks for that, Nan, I'd say, knowing she loved me but also knowing that she had a much softer spot for Ern. I loved that dog, but I did have house rules and I didn't want Nan's furniture to suffer the same fate as my own, so I had a 'no jumping on the sofa and chairs' rule, the 'lie down when told to' rule, and a 'sit, stay, here' rule – all of which went clear out of the window when he got to my nan's. I swear the only time Ern sat still when he was with her was when I came to pick him up!

On days I couldn't take Ern to work with me I missed him so much that I would often call just to see how he was: 'Nan, how's Ern?' I knew that he was more than all right, so no surprise Nan thought I was a bit crazy.

'You only called a couple of hours ago,' she'd say. 'What's wrong with you?' There was nothing wrong – I was just missing my dog, my best mate. I didn't expect to feel like that about a dog or foresee the overwhelming sense of responsibility towards him that was creeping into my life.

I knew Ern was happy with Nan, even if he was a bit spoilt, and it was good that Nan had some company during the day so the arrangement worked well for all three of us. Despite the two different sets of house rules, Ern managed to work out who he was with Nan and revert to being a good boy when he was at home or at the office with me. Somehow, he never blurred the lines and settled into his routine as a happy dog. Happy dog: happy me.

I'd say that Ern was about six months old when he first started to show problems breathing.

Ern had been loving his walks and I loved taking him out. It was our time together and the perfect antidote to a long, rubbish day at work or being on the other end of a business flight to Eastern Europe or India. Being back with Ern was the highlight of every day and I looked forward to collecting him from Nan's, having a quick cuppa with her and then heading home with my boy.

Our walks were time for being us and a big part of our bonding, and we both needed and enjoyed a good stride out together.

But one day, Ern's breathing changed.

I hadn't noticed it while we were walking but as soon as we got home there it was, the heavy breathing, shoulders rising as if he had to really work to get the air in his lungs. And that wasn't all: Ern was lethargic and not his normal self at all. He beat me to bed that night and by the time I was ready to join him he was snoring really loudly ... and when I say snoring, I probably mean choking.

I'm a light sleeper so I heard every breath ... in and out ... in and out ... all through the night. In the end I couldn't sleep for worrying because it wasn't right. I was waiting for the morning to arrive so I could do something to help him. There was no way I was going to work the next day. We were going to the vet.

The diagnosis was a heart murmur. A minor one, and not something to over-worry about, but I needed to be aware of it. There were rules now. If I wanted to keep on top of this situation and not put Ern at risk of a heart attack, I needed to monitor his breathing when we were on our walks and not overstretch him. No taxing hikes, just even-paced strolls, especially on warm days because that's when he would have the greatest problem regulating his breathing.

As the vet was talking I started to recall some of the advice he had given to me when I first registered Ern and now it was starting to mean something. I thought it didn't apply to Ern because he was a puppy. I thought all the stuff about heart and breathing problems was preparing me for situations that I might face when Ern was older, not something we would have to deal with when he reached six months old. Although I was told not to worry, I couldn't do anything else.

I was also told to keep a close eye on Ern and manage his exercise to make sure he didn't overdo it. It distressed me to see him so breathless and I was in no rush to see that again but curbing his energy wasn't easy. Ern was a bouncy pup and as soon as he was in the park and off the lead he would bomb away like a lunatic and then run back to check on me before dashing off again to repeat the whole thing.

After that day Ern still had his crazy running sessions, but not so many, and when he stopped he took a little time to catch his breath. That was a new thing for us and although it didn't seem to bother Ern too much, it concerned me. It clearly wasn't going to go away on its own.

So there was more to having a dog than I had expected. Shock, horror – it wasn't all about me after all. For some odd reason, which I don't quite understand myself now, I hadn't thought of dog ownership as another kind of 'relationship' but I could feel the weird sense of responsibility grow into something deeper. Ern was not simply an accessory to my life; he was a big part of my life and always there for me. I moaned to him if I'd had a bad day at work, I told him everything and, without saying a word, he helped me find the answers. It was a great release for me and he didn't judge me or leave me feeling like a complete tit for misplacing my trust. He loved me anyway and always knew when I needed comfort and a man hug.

Now Ern had a problem and I needed to be everything for him. I was not going to let him down.

Promises, promises ...

We all do it, right? We convince ourselves and those around us that everything is fine even though we know that situations are, in reality, not fine at all. I was guilty of convincing myself that everything was sweet with the dog-sitting arrangement with Nan and to some extent it was; Ern was happy being with her and Nan was happy to have him for company. But when I worked a stretch of twelve-hour days, and I had to mix that with the social side of my business and weave in a trip overseas, I discovered that I wasn't having the time I wanted with Ern and we weren't getting quality time together. When it came to the weekend it couldn't have been much fun for him lazing around with me while I recovered and recharged before the whole thing started all over again.

It was time to take the blinkers off and stop running around with my fingers in my ears going 'la, la, la!' I had a serious work/dog-ownership imbalance and I needed to get it sorted.

My fairy godmother must have been listening or, as I believe, the universe, because the answer to my dilemma came out of nowhere.

My friend James 'Lockie' Lock started his career in *The Only Way Is Essex* in 2013 so I had an interest in the series through him and I had a good idea of how it worked with filming schedules and all of that. We often met in Brentwood, where all the reality action takes place, to go to the gym or have a beer, so in a small way I suppose I felt slightly 'attached' to the programme and the people if only by proxy. Nevertheless, it was still a big surprise when the offer to appear in *TOWIE* came my way.

By the time the production team had finished talking my head was spinning. The timing was perfect. I've always had a head for business and I have learnt over the years to listen to that inner voice when it says it's time for a rethink, time for a move. I felt that the fates were conspiring to encourage me to make a serious change, and now that I had Ern's welfare to consider I realised that this was the time and definitely the opportunity.

It would be the end of twelve-hour working days and multiple trips overseas – instead I could easily cope with the two-hour filming sessions, the annual trip to Marbs (Marbella) with the cast and crew and the in-built party element. And it was set on my doorstep. I would be able to see more of Ern and do more with him and release my nan from virtually full-time dog care. I could work and be a better dad to Ern. The fates were on my side.

I joined Lockie and the rest of the cast on their summer trip to Marbs, which launched series fifteen. Marbella, summer 2015 – what a way to start! It was so different to anything else I had done in my life and, apart from the initial filming in Spain, I would be working down the road. And in my head that meant I could take Ern to work with me all the time. I had it sorted.

I recall saying to the *TOWIE* team: 'This dog is my life …' and I meant it. I think they knew how serious I was when they saw us together on set for the first time. Ern's debut on the show made him an instant hit! All he had to do was walk in the park, looking all smart and dapper alongside me in my smart casuals, and play nicely with another dog who belonged to one of the female cast members. We stood chatting with the amazing Nanny Pat and Ern looked a proper handsome man-dog. I was so proud of him. I'll admit that I was nervous for both of us. It was important that Ern made a good impression because the last thing I wanted was for him to start any agg with the other dogs in the cast. I guess that would have been an exit stage left, never to return!

I'll admit he had a bit of a shaky start (more on that later) but I was so proud of him passing his audition with flying colours and he was set to be my on-screen buddy as well as my off-screen shadow. He was a proper scene-stealer. Even if he was only required to sit at my feet while we filmed a typical *TOWIE* conversation piece you could sense that people would be listening to the dialogue but looking at Ern!

Ern had a stage presence and he loved the camera. Somehow, he knew how to show his best side. I think he knew that he was handsome and didn't mind showing off if showing off was required and that fitted in perfectly on the show. Several of the *TOWIE* cast members have dogs but Ern looked like the bruiser in the bunch. To see him tanking along with Beau, the skippy little Yorkie, and the other lovely, fluffy little lapdogs was so funny. They were almost their own mini-version of the cast with their own dynamic. I always admired Ern for being his own person in the group. I suppose I saw a bit of myself in him.

I loved it when Ern was recognised in the street. It made me feel so proud. He greeted every fan with a smile and lapped up the attention and praise like a true professional. I think it's great that the dogs have their own followers on social media too. Why shouldn't they? I've often felt like the 'add on' when people approach my dogs before they say hello to me, but there's a special sense of belonging and satisfaction that goes with that. I talk to my dogs like they're human so it's only an extension of that. Ern had a special way with people and I was happy to share him. Having Ern at my side was like having a version of myself that I could be proud of – even if there were times when I was not so proud of myself.

All was sweet on *TOWIE*, and I was getting the extra time with Ern just as I'd hoped. The two-hour filming sessions, photoshoots and personal appearances were much easier to handle than the extended periods of time away with my old job. Also, Nan was having a break from dog-sitting which made me feel less guilty as I knew I had been relying on her very heavily for daily support. What I hadn't considered was how a lack of routine would affect Ern. It was another lesson to learn the hard way for me: dogs, I've since discovered, are like children. They need the reassurance of a routine because without it every pick-up and drop-off feels chaotic to them, like their dad is being taken away.

It didn't take long for the cracks to show. Taking Ern to filming wasn't always practical or possible so my lovely nan stepped in to welcome Ern to her home again and we muddled along with the new way of doing things. But very quickly I started to notice a change in Ern's behaviour and I could piece together what this new, unsettled life was doing to him. Although we had plenty of down-time, which meant long periods together, the downside was that when we were apart Ern suffered separation anxiety: he was biting his paws and didn't eat at all until I came to collect him. Everything was working well for me, but the days were upside down for him to the point that he didn't know if or when I was leaving him, coming back to him or if he was going to work with me.

Perhaps I just hadn't thought it through. Without a doubt, what we had was better than before but I needed to tweak it a little. I explained to Ernest: 'This is how we earn our living now, so we just need a new routine. We're both going through the same thing, mate, but it will be fine. I promise you.' And I knew that it would be fine. All Ern needed to help him ride this wave of change was a constant. Something that was there for him 100 per cent of the time, sharing this new lifestyle. Something to stop his world rocking every time I couldn't be around. Perhaps that constant could be another dog?

As fate would have it, my job delivered the answer. When the *TOWIE* team filmed an episode at a rescue centre down the road I wasn't looking for a dog but they landed me with an armful of Frenchie puppies and I could feel my heart melting. It was a scene with Ferne, and we're really good mates, so she knew how worried I was about Ern being lonely and that it was preying on my mind a lot at the time. I don't know if Ferne meant to set the seed in my head but when she asked me if I was going to adopt one of the pups I could feel something click into place. The little guys were so cute – all blue-fawn and adorable.

When you're filming for a segment that lasts only a few minutes in an episode it can take hours when other scenarios are being shot around you on the same day. Sometimes, this will mean a lot of waiting around which can be a bit frustrating – but not that day because

I was in heaven. I had plenty of time with the little ones who, when they weren't sucking my fingers and my shirt, were fast asleep on my lap. Looking back, I guess the deal was done right there and then. And once an idea is planted in my head I find it difficult to let go. That must be the terrier in me! And, what's more, I was convinced that I had hit on the answer to Ern's behavioural problems. If Ern had a constant companion, he wouldn't be lonely and most likely wouldn't be anxious or distressed because he would have a playmate to share the experience with.

I had to find out more about the dogs and, more importantly, all there was to know about rehoming a rescue dog. This time, if I decided it was right for me and for Ern, I would be going into dog ownership with my eyes wide open.

I decided to take myself back to the dog shelter, to find out more and get my head around the idea of rehoming rather than going to a breeder. To be honest I hadn't considered taking on a rescue dog before but then I don't think I expected to find Frenchies up for adoption. The kennel staff were so good to me and so helpful. I must have sounded a right muppet asking so many questions about the centre's work and how the dogs came to be there.

If there's one thing I remember about going into the centre, it's the noise! The dogs go crazy when you enter the kennel block. I don't speak dog but it's like they're all going: 'Pick me! Choose me! Oi, come 'ere mate!' I was looking all over the place at these great dogs, large and small, all desperate to be noticed. There were around a hundred dogs in for rehoming in that centre alone, and they have twenty rehoming centres in Britain which adds up to over two thousand puppies and dogs in their care nationwide. I visited in the autumn, ahead of their Christmas 'rush'. It's over the holiday periods that staff expect to see more dogs needing their help. That's when old dogs are replaced by puppies, and others are abandoned because they are no longer cute or owners have discovered they simply cost too much to feed and care for and have just become an inconvenience. Too much trouble. It was an absolute revelation to me. So bloody sad and just another reminder that people can be selfish and crap.

Human beings, eh? I've often said, and not been ashamed to say, that I prefer dogs to most people purely because with dogs what you see is what you get, and they don't play games unless they involve a ball or a squeaky toy. I can only describe people who harm animals as sub-human. To me they don't qualify to be included in the human race, or breathe the same air as the rest of us. I listened to the lovely staff at the centre telling me the stories behind some of the dogs and I was on the verge of tears.

I saw sad and lost-looking elderly dogs who you would rather see lying in front of the fire relaxing and enjoying their 'retirement', but I was told that lots of older dogs find themselves looking for a new home when their owners pass away or have to move into a care home. I didn't realise that so few care homes allow people to take their pets with them and that's something I don't understand when a pet is often that person's only companion. And there are so many younger dogs who have lost their families due to changes in circumstances – perhaps down to a job loss or having to move into rented accommodation where pets are not allowed. Dogs, I've learnt, are often the innocent victims of unfortunate human events. The kind of unforeseen life change that could happen to any of us at any time. I knew that I was going to hug Ern a bit closer when I got home.

And there were the others, their soulful eyes meeting mine through the walls of the new glass kennels. They'd not only had their trust broken; it had been well and truly trashed. They had been abused, abandoned and treated so cruelly that you would expect them to bite your hand off, not greet you with a smile and a licky-kiss. If I had been treated like that I'm sure I would be one angry bastard and no one would want to come near me! Clearly, these brave dogs are made of bigger and better stuff than me. I felt humbled that after all their suffering they could still show affection to people and be so willing to trust again. Totally amazing, every single one of them.

And there they were – the Frenchie pups I'd met during the filming … and that special one who had drooled on me. I remembered him when I got home after the filming because my shirt was still damp from his slobbery muzzle resting on my arm. He was just shy of three months old, blue-fawn and a nice guy. I had to hear his story. What poor excuse for a human had put this little guy in a place like this?

I know I wasn't looking to bring home another dog on this particular day as I'd wanted to do more research first, but I couldn't leave the centre without knowing more about this little one. How could I have known that when I asked about this special pup I was opening a door to a whole new phase in my life?

The puppy's journey had started three months earlier in Hungary. He had been born to a mother who was most likely just one of many Frenchie bitches imprisoned in one of many Hungarian puppy farms. She would have been permanently pregnant, having two litters each year, and feeding each litter of six or more pups at a time. She would have had little food and no veterinary care. The bitches would be bred until they died or ended up being dumped or disposed of because they could no longer supply the demands of their keepers. This intensive farming for commercial gain continues in eastern Europe, far away from the UK, without any legislation to control the breeding, selling and transportation of the dogs, despite the numbers involved and the obvious cruelty. And that's just the start of the story. What I heard next made me so angry I could hardly contain myself.

I'm looking at this little pup, his chubby little grey body lying flat-out asleep on his belly and I'm being told that he would have been taken from his mother before he was even eight weeks old, drugged, packed into a small crate with other drugged puppies, with no access to food or water, shoved into the back of a van for a journey of over a thousand miles to be offered up for sale in the lucrative Christmas market in the UK.

I reckon someone must have been looking over this lot of puppies because when the loaded van reached the port of Dover it was intercepted by the authorities and the puppies were handed over to rescue centers. They were the lucky ones, but I was told that the fate of many more is very grim. Puppy smuggling is big business and each vehicle that manages to sneak its illegal cargo through border control contains thousands of pounds' worth of potential sales.

It's only in the past three years that animal organisations have been allowed to step in and rescue the seized cargo of pups. Before that the puppies faced being put to sleep, or another journey of hundreds of miles back again to an unknown destination, and God knows what and who at the end of it all.

Some of the puppies are too sick to survive the journey to the UK; others arrive in a desperate state both physically and psychologically. Having only ever known a cage as a home, having been kept quiet with drugs, denied human contact and good food, these pups are still incredibly trusting. When the port authorities take them out of the cages, they surrender to their care. It's bloody amazing. I was in tears hearing this and I'm not ashamed to admit it.

It turns out that the majority of puppies are illegally transported from Hungary, Latvia and Poland and smuggled into the UK via the Eurotunnel, arriving in Folkestone, or on ferry carriers to Dover. Packed into vans or hidden away in the boots of cars, they arrive in the early morning destined to be sold to dealers, known as third-party sellers, being kept in service-station car parks or laybys and other anonymous locations ready to begin their next journey into the hands of an unsuspecting owner who believes they have found their perfect puppy. I know that feeling of finding the perfect puppy – I felt it with Ern – but the difference is I had seen him with his mum and in his home surroundings with his siblings. It had never occurred to me, until now, how incredibly important that was. I kind of took it for granted.

I'd never heard of the puppy-smuggling trade but now that I had I wanted to know a lot more and how I could campaign to stop it.

First thing – the little drooling puppy, did he need a home?

Yes, his carer said – he was looking for a home.

I wondered what Ernest would say when I told him all about this little guy.

As I walked out of the building I was planning how to tell Ern what I had in mind. Taking on another dog would be a big decision, but I had already booked an appointment to go back to the rescue centre so Ern could meet the little guy, and if all went well then the puppy was ours. But if it was a disaster I would have to find another way to help the pup be rehomed while still respecting Ern's feelings. I had to put Ern first. This time it was all about him.

I decided that bedtime was the best time to talk this through with Ernest. I felt nervous and I've no idea why! Well, that's not true, the reason was that I liked the little puppy I had seen, and I wanted Ern to like him too. As we lay on the bed I stroked Ern's lovely ears and explained that I'd seen the little guy, he was a blue-fawn Frenchie and he was a puppy with a lot of love to give and who would need a lot of love from both of us in return. By this time Ern had manoeuvred himself into his usual position, stretched out at the bottom of the bed. I'm not sure at what point he fell asleep because I was so busy explaining but when I finally heard him snore I realised that I had been talking to myself.

There was only one way this puppy was going to be right for us and that was if he was right for Ern. I had some time to wait anyway while the little one was being taken through his paces by his carers at the centre. In fact, my puppy (I'll call him that for now) was one of the first on the scheme which the centre introduced to make sure the puppies seized at the ports are seen through quarantine, health-checked and placed with a regional rehoming centre for socialisation and support to find a responsible owner. This time I could be a responsible owner. At least I had done my homework and now the rest was up to Ern.

It was November 2015 when I returned to the local centre with Ern in tow. I'm guessing that when he saw me putting his dog coat in the car he thought we were going on a walk but he didn't look disappointed when he jumped out to be met by the crazy noise of the dog shelter chorus. I couldn't help thinking that one of those barks could belong to the little guy we were there to meet. I was really excited about seeing him again and remember skipping along to one of the rehab rooms to wait for him to be brought in.

Moments later, there he was in the arms of one of the carers. What a top geezer! He smiled. I'm absolutely positive he smiled at me. He looked a bit shy and timid but as soon as I took him in my arms he snuggled into my body and made himself comfortable under my armpit. His little body relaxed into mine with a sigh as if he had made his choice to stay. For me, that was it. But what about Ern?

There was something about this little one. It was the way he looked at me. We connected in some way and I found myself saying, hopefully not out loud: 'Please, Ern, like this dog. Please … please … please …' I had already decided that if this meeting between the two dogs didn't go well I still wanted to be involved in the puppy's care and do all I could to help him find the best home. I knew his story now and he had suffered enough already in his short life. If I had anything to do with it there would be no more bad stuff for him. I had an overwhelming need to protect him and he wasn't even mine. One last and most important hurdle – it was time to introduce him to Ern. The pup's four blue paws had only just touched the floor and Ern bounced up to the little guy and gave him a sniff. That was it. The moment when it could have all gone wrong ... but everything went perfectly. Ern gained a little blue-fawn shadow who never left his side.

And then we were three.

The centre had already checked me out and they were happy that the puppy would be going into a safe and healthy environment. I guess they had met me enough times by then to get the measure of me and ask their questions. Ern had behaved himself too, so we qualified to take the puppy home.

If I was worried about the puppy tearing round the flat and destroying everything, I didn't need to be. Believe me, there was nothing 'speedy' about this puppy. If he had one favourite pastime when he first arrived home, it was sleeping. He slept really well and at any time of the day, no matter what was going on around him. He fell asleep in the car, on photoshoots, during *TOWIE* filming, on people's laps, on random chairs and sofas ... anywhere he happened to come to a standstill. Sleep. And when he wasn't asleep he was busy growing into his big personality.

What's in a name? Well, in Eric's case, this little pup's name just ... arrived. Eric came from nowhere. It just suddenly came into use one day and stuck. Eric is very much an Eric, know what I mean? Which to me is a nice bloke, a fun bloke and, in my Eric's case, a bit daft too! He answered to it right away and the new name just happened without any fuss or bother. I made sure that I called him by name at every opportunity and gave him lots of fuss every time he came to me so 'recall' was never a problem.

Although lots of people assume that I named my two Frenchies after the famous comedy double-act, Morecambe and Wise (Eric and Ern), I didn't. Although when people kept asking about the names and I realised who they were talking about I don't think I could have chosen better handles for my own four-legged double-act because, together, they were a couple of comedians. And on his own, Eric can't help being an entertainer even if it is accidental.

When I think of Eric making his debut on *TOWIE* I kind of smile and cringe at the same time! Of course, by this time Ern was well established on the set from the third programme in series fifteen and had gained himself a reputation for being a true professional. He had no problem looking to camera and could always strike a typical Frenchie pose as he had the classic square head, bold shoulders, bat ears and wrinkled nose. If Ern had been human, he would have been an excellent actor. If Eric, however, had been born human he would have made a great taxi driver who loved chatting to all the people, helping you get where you wanted to go but not wanting to be the centre of attention. Ern knew all the moves; his timing was excellent, and he followed stage direction better than the rest of us. So, when I introduced Eric to the cast and crew I'm guessing they were expecting a dog out of the same mould.

Perhaps I should have warned them that although they had met Ern and he was a Frenchie, meeting Eric would be a whole new experience. As it happens, the first chance I had to introduce him to everyone was at the photoshoot for series sixteen which brought the entire cast together, all the guys poshed-up in our Sunday best suits and the girls sparkling in their evening gowns. It was a pukka occasion but, as you can imagine, with dogs on set there was a whiff of danger in the air.

Ern and Eric weren't the only dogs taking part; other cast members were being photographed with their four-legged friends too, so it was quite an operation to get everyone ready and the dogs on their best behaviour. I knew Ern could be trusted to behave, but Eric? He was just a puppy then and virtually everything was new to him. I could say two things for certain: one was that he would be good with the people, and two – this was the dodgy bit – he would want to make friends with the other dogs. He's a sociable fella, my Eric, but this was not an occasion to go around sniffing bottoms. There was a distinct fear that success or failure of my new career in telly was now in Eric's paws.

As always with these big photoshoots it was a marathon day. Patience and tempers were stretched and still the job had to be done and smiles fixed. I had bought new leads and harnesses for the boys and they looked so smart. The Wolfpack was out and making a statement and I don't mind telling you that it felt amazing.

Suddenly, after hours of waiting around and the hair and make-up folk dashing between us, it was our turn. Ern was raring to go. He was just waiting for me to give him the nudge. And Eric? Eric was asleep! Truthfully, he was so soundly asleep that we couldn't wake him up for love nor money. He had gone to the Land of Nod good and proper and when that happens to Eric that's all you have to work with – a sleeping dog. We tried to tempt him with food and tickles and all that, but he was actually snoring. There was no chance that the photographer was going to get that 'Essex bloke and his geezer dogs' shot because Eric was out for the count. The best I could manage for the photo was to rest his head on my hand.

Thanks a bunch, Eric!

I was mortified but then I'm his dad, so I forgave him in a heartbeat and everyone else just thought it was hilarious! I think dogs bring out the best in people and, as far as I can see, this is proven day after day. Dogs can lead by example and show us the way. All we need to do is watch and learn from them.

When Eric first came home I was afraid that Ern would turn all territorial and make life difficult for him, at least for a while. But Ern was the perfect gentleman and the perfect big brother rolled into one.

Ern was a natural leader and it was under his guidance that Eric perfected his toilet training and learnt how to behave at home, at work and when they stayed with my nan. Eric just mirrored Ern's every move. Well, most of his moves. They didn't always stick to the plan, but you have to put that down to the mischief gene in the breed – they're fun guys after all. Generally though, Eric moved in Ern's shadow every day and the two were inseparable. In a way this left me to be the leader in our emerging Wolfpack.

At home they had their own beds, but they chose to sleep on mine. They had their own water and food bowls and never ate out of each other's. Even if one of them left food, the other one never moved in to mop it up. And as for the array of toys that have now ended up on the dog bed in the living room that has never been slept on, they have all been ignored in favour of plastic drink bottles. Apparently, the best dog toy in the universe – according to Ern and Eric. They will have several on the go at any one time and as soon as you offer them a new one that bottle then becomes their favourite. I could have saved myself a few quid if I'd known that a plastic drinks bottle was all the entertainment they wanted!

It's not easy being the leader, I discovered. There's a massive responsibility that goes with the role and although I considered myself 'in charge' of my Frenchies I was constantly reminded that I was also part of their entertainment package. But I knew I would do everything I had to do to make sure my boys were happy.

My newfound responsibility as Wolfpack leader changed my personality and made me grow up a lot. My nan was the first to notice the difference it made in me. Now my nan has always made a fuss of me. I've always known that I'm her blue-eyed boy and that's a very special feeling whatever your age. In my nan's eyes I still can't do anything wrong and in having dogs, I did everything right.

Nan fell in love with Ern the first time she met him. She said it was like having another grandson. When Eric came along I felt like I had presented her with a third grandchild! She couldn't have been happier. After that whenever I called her she would ask, 'How's my Ern and my Eric?' It really was a lovely thing to share with my nan and she was so happy with me for choosing to share my life with those two Frenchies. They helped me to show her that I was getting my act together and that I could be responsible for someone else and not just myself.

So, this was life at home with Ern and Eric: the Wolfpack. When we weren't at work we were going for walks in the park, visiting friends or chilling out at home. They were my family and my best friends, and I couldn't have been happier. Our social media friends took my Frenchies to their hearts and put them in the spotlight. Luckily it was the kind of public appearance that Eric could deal with because it didn't involve being filmed. You see, unlike Ern, Eric is quite shy. At least he's camera shy. Maybe he knows that he has wonky teeth? Whatever it is, Eric is a reluctant star.

While Ern took the job of actor seriously, Eric likes to act the clown and mess about. He can't help it. It's like chaos follows him around. For anyone who remembers the comedy sketch featuring Morecambe and Wise where

Eric is at the piano playing 'all the right notes but not necessarily in the right order', that's how some days can go with my Eric. He's his own person and I love the way he keeps me on my toes!

Before I had a dog, I had heard about walks in the park that didn't always go to plan, with dogs eating the bread put out for the ducks and even running after the ducks, but I had never heard of the ducks terrifying dogs. That's until I witnessed Eric's attempt to make friends with a duck and her ducklings. We were filming in Brentwood park and I had noticed the ducks by the lake but thought no more about it. Normally the ducks don't bother with dogs, but swans are a different matter. I would always keep away from them, especially when they have cygnets, but ducks? No problem ... or so I thought. I didn't reckon on Eric plodding up to the little group of ducklings on the edge of the lake and nuzzling into them with his snuffly snout! He probably would have got away with it if their mum hadn't been watching the whole thing! When she laid eyes on Eric there was a proper commotion. She hissed and flapped her wings at him but still he didn't move for a few seconds. He was probably thinking she would change her mind or something! Then, the penny obviously dropped, and he kicked up his heels and ran – with the duck just inches behind. There went Eric – tail between his legs and a duck chasing after him!

Embarrassed? You bet!

Two bowls, two beds, and a doubly huge pile of toys remain to remind me daily that we were a family. When I first brought Eric home I wondered if I would have room in my heart for two dogs because I couldn't imagine loving Eric as much as I already loved Ern, but it was all there inside me, ready to give. My Frenchies, the Wolfpack, completed me and in the nine months we three had together I learnt so much and came so very far. I can see now that having the dogs was just the start of the long journey for me and I had a long way to go but I was accompanied by the pad of paws alongside me, every step of the way.

I now appreciate that a responsible potential dog owner, who had done all their homework, would have been prepared for the pee, wee and chew situation with Ern. I was not prepared but I was lucky that the 'difficult' stuff didn't last long because Ern had been house-trained and socialised by the breeder before he came home with me. In other words, Ern knew the basics, but he was thrown by the change in home environment and with some patience (and distraction) from me he calmed down and settled into our routine. In character, Ern was a solid geezer and his background was traceable and he had the Kennel Club papers to prove his pedigree.

Eric, on the other hand, was a whole different story. He was a rescue dog and, as often is the case with rescues, their story unfolds with you as you live with them and love them. I asked plenty of questions at the rehoming centre to get the best possible picture of Eric's background, but I appreciated that they couldn't tell me a lot as they didn't know his mother or his brothers and sisters either. They could only assume that he had survived the usual dirty and squalid conditions of a puppy farm in Eastern Europe. He was one of many, but he has his own funny little ways, and some are clues to his past. Eric, for instance, gets excited when he smells tobacco. Nothing else makes him behave that way. It's because he associates it with his time in the van travelling from Hungary as a smuggled puppy. He, along with his mates, were hidden amongst cases of tobacco. The smell brings it all back to him. Poor little lad.

I was lucky that I had all that Ern taught me to apply to Eric's 'growing up'. Could I have done it all better?

Yes, without doubt. If I freeze-frame and backtrack a little I will confess to not reading up on what it takes to be a fully functioning responsible dog owner. I just jumped straight in. I should have researched the breed – French bulldogs – and known a little more about their history and breeding and not just the different colours available. If I had I would have known that there was more to their flat features, bulging eyes, long backs and skin wrinkles than meets the eye. Breathing, heart and dodgy spine problems seem almost built in to the breed, and the skin folds and shallow eye sockets make regular bathing essential to avoid irritation or infection. It's sad that the features that we think make them adorable are also the things that can, if they are not looked after, cause discomfort and suffering.

Poor Eric had problems with his skin when he was rescued, although he received the best of care to clear up the issues during his rehabilitation. I learnt how to look after Ern's skin to save him from difficulties and I'm happy to bathe Eric's eyes and little folds every day to make sure he is comfortable. It's just part of our little beauty – or should I say 'man-maintenance' – routine! Not everyone who takes on a Frenchie knows about these things and I've discovered that dogs can find themselves in rescue homes when owners let the problems get out of hand and become expensive to treat. All this must be thought of when taking on a rescue dog whose problems are not always in your face from day one. Every day can bring a new revelation. I think that must be part of the challenge and the reward all at the same time.

After I saw my first Frenchie in the street that day I began to see them all over the place. It's always the way when you have something fixed in your mind that you want to buy, like a certain make or colour of car or watch: suddenly it is everywhere. I looked at pictures of the dogs on the internet and the list of Kennel Club-registered breeders, but it never occurred to me that the popularity of the breed was so great that demand could exceed the supply. Why is it that it never takes long for some greedy individual to come up with an illegal, profit-maximising way to meet that demand? Puppy smuggling is cruel and all about money and nothing to do with animal welfare. The third-party sellers, no matter if they are legal or illegal, allow this to happen and even encourage it to continue. They advertise online, selling pups who have been taken early from their mum in a place well away from where they were born. If I hadn't visited the rehoming centre to find out more about rescue dogs I probably wouldn't have discovered this sinister side of the pet trade.

Rescuing a dog is all about second chances and, in my book, everyone and every dog deserves that. You don't give up on someone just because they're a bit broken. I know that in his own way Ernest had already rescued me and then, together, we rescued Eric. I came to realise that every prospective dog owner should have knowledge about the dog they want and top that off with a dollop of patience. Me? I got there along the way, with a little help from my friend Ern. He helped me, and he taught me so much.

Life with Ern and Eric opened my eyes to some brand-new sensations and sparked some new aspirations and hopes. The nine months I had them together was the best time in my life.

We were a proper family. We were the Wolfpack. The sweetest thing ever.

Chapter 2

Who Do You Think You Are?

The history of the Frenchie

MY MUM IS a Bow-Bell Cockney. She is the real deal because she was born within earshot of the church bells of St Mary-le-Bow in the Cheapside district of London. I'm proud to say that I come from a dynasty of true East Enders who have jellied eels and pie and mash in their blood. That said, I was born in Harlow, grew up in Harlow and now the hub of my life and work is in Brentwood so I am a proud Essex boy, heart and soul, and could quite rightly claim 'the only way is Essex' as my family motto. Maybe the words could be written over the front door or maybe it's something I could have tattooed on my chest. Only joking! Although, when I think about it, the ink on my skin gives so many clues to who I am, where I'm from and, more than anything, where I'm heading.

I'll be honest, there's not a lot of my skin that is free from ink. It's probably quicker to tell you that I only have my left leg and my stomach free for any more major artwork. So far everything I have on my body carries a message that I want to keep close to me as a permanent reminder of who I am and what I believe in and, if I look at it all closely and think about it carefully, my skin tells a story all of its own. Mind you, I don't want you to think that every tattoo has been carefully thought out because I am wearing some pretty bad decisions and plenty that could have done with some more thought behind them. Let's just say that I grew wiser with every tattoo along the way.

I was eighteen years old and only just legal when I first set foot inside a tattoo parlour. I couldn't wait to get that ink on my body. I had wanted a tatt for so long and this was the day my dream was going to come true. I was buzzing with excitement after such a long wait and now I was in the place I didn't want to wait around any more. I proudly showed the tattooist my sketch.

The design had just come into my head. Just floated in there, inspired by native American art because I was well into all that in my teens. I read a lot about the native tribes and their spirituality and deep connection with animal symbolism, which crossed over with my love of wolves. All of this captured my imagination and I started to mentally sketch out the tattoo that I wanted to have on my left arm. This was going to be a piece of me, at eighteen, that would be with me forever. I liked the thought of that. It wasn't until years later that my nan said that this first tattoo, of a native American warrior, resembled one of her own drawings from a long time ago, a drawing that she had never shown to a single soul. Her words made the hair on the back of my neck stand high. 'But Nan, we've never spoken about this before. How can that happen? How did I know?' I'm very close to my nan but that was spooky and if the connection was telepathic or something else along those lines, then that sketch was sent to me in my sleep. Maybe it came from my past but a little piece of my past that I didn't know about or, more likely, had forgotten about.

My nan is a spiritualist and a healer too, but I didn't know this until much later in my life. Once we started to talk about it I realised that the clues were always there in her house, so I would have been surrounded by them all as a child. The feathery dream-catchers hanging in doorways and coloured crystals on windowsills and in cabinets are all signs and symbols of the spirits that guide and guard us. Nan has a gift for all of that and I think I understand it more now than I ever did. She has always watched over me, but now I know that there is something more to it and that she is no doubt at the root of my sensitivity to the symbols and signs that accompany us on our journey through life.

My tatts didn't always have a meaning at the time I had them done. Some would just come to me when I was in the chair and then, years later, they have suddenly made sense. Almost as if they were painted into the mix to be warnings or guidance in the future. You know what I mean? I know it sounds weird, I really do, but in the months after losing Ernest I looked for signs and symbols of all kinds to help and guide me, and the tatts have thrown up some interesting and inspiring thoughts. It's as if they are an extension of myself, a kind of portable, personal vision board that I have created to develop who I am and what I'm aiming for in life. In my case that's to find peace of mind and unconditional love to fill the gap left by Ern's passing. I guess it's deep stuff but, since Nan told me about her sketch, I was bound to start looking for messages in every spot of ink on my body.

Queen of Hearts, King of Hearts on my right leg, half a skeleton on my shoulder, flowers with chains and padlocks ... are there keys for all the padlocks? A skull on my back held in two hands and a pocket watch showing time passing. If time stands still, and it all goes wrong, we still need love. I thought all of that was just dramatic inking until I thought: 'I'm approaching my thirtieth birthday and the message in this has to be – get on and do those things you've always wanted to do. And do them now.' It's like the old saying: this is life, not a dress rehearsal ... In other words: 'It's time to get your 'aris (arse) off the ground, mate!'

There are a fair few characters dangling from my family tree, all good hard-working people, who would tell me that anything is possible – if you want it badly enough. My nan's brother, Uncle Ernest, was a proper role model and a man-mountain to boot. Nothing would have stood in his way and if it had tried he would have burst through it like the East End version of the Incredible Hulk! It's good to remember the calibre of the people you are related to and who share the same blood. It's a good thing to go back to when you're feeling a bit lost for answers. A good old chat with my nan will usually put me right. She has a gift for that too. I think by naming Ernest after Nan's brother I've managed to keep the warm and burly spirit of Uncle Ern in our hearts.

I love that feeling of belonging and, although it annoyed me when I was younger, I can now see why older relatives look at children in the family and say: 'Oh look, he's got your eyes ... and Granddad's nose ... and those ears must belong to your side of the family ...' You get the gist? Well, it's just the same when you look at some dog breeds. If you think about it, the 'look' of some dogs has really changed over the years: bigger heads, smaller heads, tails, no tails, taller, smaller, hairier, non-shedding, wrinklier, smoother, curlier, straighter ... and so it goes on to fit the fashion of the day. And when I eventually started to read

about the history of the French bulldog, I could see Ern
and Eric as stars in what is a real rags-to-riches story of
the fighting dog turned lapdog.

It's not easy to see much of the wolf in Eric. If all
domestic dogs are descended from these majestic wild
creatures, then the strains of the lupine were running
very low when they reached him. Eric has about as much
ferocity in him as candy floss on a stick but his family
tree – that's the Frenchie family tree – introduces some
members of the bulldog breed that you really wouldn't
want to meet down a smog-filled back alley in Queen
Victoria's East End.

Imagine a group of men huddled together at the end of
a street, voices raised, beer flowing and money changing
hands, which often meant there was something there to
lay a bet on. Cock-fighting, bull-baiting and dog-fights
were commonplace in working-class communities where
the beer was cheap and so was life. Gambling on bare-
knuckle fights and sparring dogs were cruel sports in a
hard life and they were not very well hidden from view.
Big, muscular, flat-faced bulldogs were pitted against each
other, often to the death, and even the survivor would be
torn, scarred and bloody.

This was a way of life for these dogs who were kept
lean and made mean. Even for the bulldogs kept as pets, or

more likely as scary guard dogs, it was a tough life in the ordinary working man's home where there wasn't much food going spare, and there was even less on the streets for beggars – and that's for humans and animals. It hurts me every time I read anything like this about cruelty to dogs because, without fail, I see Ern and Eric in that time and that place. I can't help it. It's real and it did happen. And in some parts of the world it is still happening.

I'm no expert but becoming a dog owner and then losing Ernest plunged me into wanting to know all about Frenchies and animal welfare. There's plenty to read if you want to learn about cruelty to animals, especially if you delve into the dusty archives. Be warned: it will make you extremely angry. Back in Victorian London, on street level, there didn't seem to be any respect for animals, including working horses or pet dogs, none of whom had status or protection. Finding out what happened to them makes depressing, grim reading. But then there are some disgusting human beings on the earth so what can we expect?

In fact, the bulldog breeds have been involved in 'blood sports' for a very, very long time. Way before the Frenchie came about, as we know them anyway, the ancient Greeks used an ancestor of the French bulldog for hunting. The Molossian tribe started this off in Greece and then the Phoenicians, who traded worldwide, made the breed popular everywhere they went. We Brits developed the mastiff breed out of the dogs who landed on our shores and it was usually this breed of dog that artists later captured in paintings – all muscle, teeth and drool.

So, when did the little French bulldog, as we know and love them, come into all this?

Well, when the long arm of the law finally came down on illegal dog-fighting in 1835, the bulldog breeds were crossed with terriers and pugs to make them smaller and easier to live with around the house. Various versions of 'toy' bulldogs started to appear in dog shows up and down the country, where people saw them, liked them and wanted one.

While the rich folk fell over themselves trying to get their hands on a miniature bulldog, new technology of the day was forcing some elements of the Victorian working class to move abroad for work before they died of starvation. With the Industrial Revolution in full swing in Britain, certain groups of artisan workers were forced to take their skills abroad where the old ways were still valued, and many took their little bulldogs with them for company and probably security and protection too. Unemployed Nottingham lace makers who took their skills to Normandy get the first big mention in the Frenchie family history because they are credited with mixing their miniature bulldogs with the local French 'ratters'. This is probably where the 'ear' thing came into the breed, alongside the calm and friendly temperament that we all know and love. The English were happy to send over the dogs they thought were too small and any they thought had the unacceptably big, funny ears.

It was a breed sensation! By 1860-ish, posh French society couldn't get enough of the little geezers and if reality TV had existed back then, the newly launched 'Frenchie' would have been treading the red carpet and sitting at the feet of celebrity actors, artists and singing stars of the day. There was huge demand from high society ladies to have one on their lap, especially in stylish Paris just before the turn of the twentieth century. As a result you can often see this cute little flat-faced dog taking its place in works of art by celebrated artists such as Toulouse-Lautrec and Degas. These little pups were staring out of fashionable Parisian street scenes as if they owned the gaff. Well, they certainly looked as if they belonged – and that's because they did. The basic British miniature bulldog was still in there somewhere but the French were busy making this little dog all their own, and making a lot of dosh along the way.

So that's how the words 'bulldog' and 'French' came together to turn out one of history's most successful Anglo-French 'inventions'. A bit like the roll out of Concorde, only this time it was a dog with big ears not an aircraft with a big nose!

Around this time the breeding got a little bit mixed in with more terrier and probably a bit of pug thrown in too, but it didn't seem to matter because what came out of it was the trademark rounded eyes and the tall 'bat' ears. It's what people wanted, and the breeders were giving it to them. I'm not sure we want to entirely forgive the breeders and sellers who were making all the money out of these dogs because clearly they didn't care about the health problems they were storing up in the breed. Or perhaps we could be generous and say that maybe they didn't understand that this type of breeding was going to cause long-term health issues in their dogs. Either way, these folks were on a nice little earner and weren't about to get all moral and grow a conscience when the fashion for the flatter-faced dog was at its height. And, more to the point, the people buying up the stock were the rich and famous of the day. There was no limit to what they would pay.

The Russian royal family organised for the little dogs to be sent from France and in no time the new fashionable pets were included in family photographs and taking their place in history. Our own Queen Victoria was a fan of flat-faced breeds and was very fond of 'pug dogs', especially the apricot-fawn colouring which she championed throughout the sixty-three years she was on the throne. Apparently, the Queen also created her own dynasty of pugs which she gave away to her family and friends all over Europe. I wasn't sure I liked the idea of her having over twenty pugs running all over the place but they would certainly have made her smile, so that was a good thing. And she gave something back to the breed when she put her royal weight behind the movement to ban the cruel practice of 'ear cropping' pugs, which was popular in England during her reign.

I liked another thing I read about Queen Victoria too. It really struck a chord with me because I'm still deciding how I can create a memorial to Ernest. It was about how the Queen remembered her favourite pug, Bosco, who was her closest companion after her beloved Prince Albert died. She had a small tomb built for Bosco in the gardens at Frogmore House in Windsor, very close to the Mausoleum where the Prince's body was laid to rest. Then she commissioned a bronze sculpture of the dog to sit outside her bedroom at Osborne House on the Isle of Wight. She couldn't bear to be without that dog. And

I totally understand that feeling. You see, Queen or no Queen, the loss of a pet still feels the same no matter who you are or where you live.

Even if good old Queen Vic didn't have a Frenchie, her son, Edward VIII, did. He liked his dogs – the royals don't seem to be able to get enough of them – and was usually photographed with a white terrier, but his Frenchie, Peter, sneaked into a few shots too. He looked a bit of a tearaway, so I can just imagine the royal photographer setting up a shot and the dogs all scurrying about. The little Frenchie would be doing his own thing with a big smile on his face, knowing he was messing it all up! If he was anything like Eric, that is. The royals could have done with the Erns of the Frenchie world, so they had half a chance of a good shot. Especially as they didn't have the benefit of digital cameras!

Popular in France, Austria and Germany, the Frenchie was starting to take over the world. Its reputation for friendliness, loyalty, strength and 'steadfast tenacity' made them popular with people from all walks of society. As a dog for all social classes, it was just as likely to be seen in the arm of a Parisienne brothel madame as royalty or a member of the American aristocracy.

In fact, all of us Frenchie owners have our American cousins to thank for determining the breed standard that stopped any more messing with their already perfect features. American tourists visiting France in the later 1800s took the Frenchie breed to their hearts – and back to America. As a result, it was the Americans who set the seal on the breed standard – the recognised characteristics that make up each individual breed – and made the final decision on the ears.

American dog lovers had been importing the English bulldog for years but when the new French bulldog came along they couldn't get enough of it. By 1885, they set up their own breeding programme and the 'ladies who lunch' – the Chelsea set of the day – quickly surrounded themselves with the fashionable little dogs. A year later, they took them along to the Westminster Kennel Club Dog Show – the US version of Britain's famous dog show, Crufts – for the first time. The Frenchie wowed the crowds and caused a sensation. They also caused a bit of agg, thanks to the judge, a Mr Sven Feltstein, who only chose winners with the old-fashioned 'rose ears' that folded at the tip. The ladies were so angry with him for openly snubbing their bat-eared beauties that they formed the French Bull Dog Club of America and established the breed standard, which stated for the first time that the 'erect bat ear' is the correct type. The ears have it.

By the early 1900s Frenchie pups were changing hands for over $3,000 and enjoying a life of luxury in the homes of the American aristocracy such as the Rockefellers and founders of financial institutions like J. P. Morgan. By the time the American Kennel Club recognised the French bulldog breed in 1898 it was the fifth most popular breed in America. And the nickname, Frenchie, became recognised all over the world.

Stars of the silent movies of the day were keen to get their hands on a Frenchie and welcome them into their homes in the Hollywood Hills. Top-billing actors including Douglas Fairbanks and the music hall star Gertie Millar had Frenchies. Considering Millar was the most photographed female performer in Edwardian musical theatre, a picture of her with her dog would probably have had a similar reaction to one of Madonna with hers today.

While the American Kennel Club opened its arms wide to welcome the Frenchie, the Brits held back – but not for too long. By 1906 the British Kennel Club decided to embrace the Frenchie name and breed spec. The dogs were so popular by now that they must have decided that it was silly to carry on resisting.

I read a funny thing about the Kennel Club ladies coming up with the idea of collecting dog hair to spin to make socks for soldiers in the trenches on the Western Front during the First World War. What a brilliant idea, and it was successful with hairier dogs like the Pekingese. But it just made me think how they would have got on collecting Frenchie hair. My guess is – not very well!

They did really well though as sailors' travelling companions on merchant ships and as faithful ships' mascots during the war. Can you imagine the little guys bustling around below decks in a warship or a merchant ship being everyone's friend, sneaking food and trying to kip in someone's hammock? I can – and all I can say is it's a good job they were compact-sized dogs in a place where there is no room to spare. When I was told about this I worried how many didn't make it back home. Ern hated going out in the rain so I'm not sure how happy he would have been on the ocean waves! He would have loved the captive audience though and all the fuss and attention on offer. That would have been heaven for a Frenchie … at least for a while.

Dogs became film stars after the First World War and lots of people would have heard about the German shepherd, Rin Tin Tin, who was rescued by an American soldier from a battlefield in France. He went on to make twenty-seven successful movies in Hollywood and only Lassie, the faithful collie, was able to give Rin Tin Tin a run for his money, but that was later in the 1950s and 60s. At that time Frenchies were more likely to find fame in the arms of a film star rather than on the screen. Just think what Marilyn Monroe and her Frenchie would have done for the breed's popularity today!

Now you know I like a good suit, so I was pleased to learn that the fashion designer Yves Saint Laurent was a Frenchie fan too. His dynasty of dogs – all called Moujik – began with an unusually moody Frenchie who, by the sound of it, was a bit of a show-off and an attention seeker! Maybe he didn't like sharing his owner with the team at the fashion house in Paris. One thing's for sure, he didn't like the models much as he always drooled on their clothes, which didn't go down very well. A Frenchie with an artistic temperament. That's so funny and so Frenchie. Every one of them a little unique. I love that about them.

Celebrity owners from the world of film, fashion and music – is this starting to sound familiar?

It's as if the whole family history of the Frenchie has gone full circle and, just over a century after gaining proper recognition as a breed, they have hit the headlines today for the same reasons. Once again, they are the popular choice and it's easy to see why because they are just so adorable!

Someone once said that the Frenchie is 'like a clown in the cloak of a philosopher' and I'll go along with that. They do look funny. Even Ern – for all his party-boy bravado turned big-brother seriousness – still had the bat-eared bulldog look about him. And as for Eric? Well, he has the clown in his nature and he attracts chaos but I always forgive him for that because he makes me laugh. Since we lost Ern, the lad has stepped up to my side. I don't expect the same amount of words of wisdom and knowing looks that I got from Ern but he's there for me and he listens – and we have fun!

Frenchies are funny guys and they are also calm and intelligent. They are the kind of 'people' you want around you when the world kicks dust in your face because you know they will say: 'It's OK … come and sit with me and we'll chat if you want to, relax if you need to and I'll generally be there for you.' In other words, they always know what you need from them. It's like a sixth sense.

I love the history of the Frenchie because it shows you how magical they are. They bustle on through everything, taking it all in their stride and doing it all with a smile. They bring out the best in people – Eric is still doing that for me. I think one of their greatest qualities is that they are classless. There are no borders with Frenchies. They are the Cinderella of the dog world: with ancestors street-fighting in Victorian slums and chasing vermin in rat-infested French workshops, they rose out of the dirt to dine at the tables of royalty and in the company of the landed gentry – and high-class prostitutes. These guys are social class heroes.

I think it's really interesting that today's couch-potato Frenchie is a direct descendant of the once super-sporty bulldog. And also, it's a reminder that dog-fighting was once a 'sport' supported by the rich and the poor. It's horrific even to think about that now especially when I think of Ern and Eric and see peace-loving, affectionate little pals who just want a cuddle and to spend time with you.

But it's true that as a breed they are very adaptable. No longer sporting dogs and happier being lapdogs, the Frenchie has been shrunk to fit modern lifestyles. They are just as happy stomping about on a country estate as a council estate – as long as they are loved. They have been 'designed' to fit in with us – and they do. This probably all goes back to their breeding and the mix of nationalities that were keen to see them succeed, such as the French, Germans, Brits and Americans. They are a true collaborative success. A designer dog for today – passed down from a century ago. If *TOWIE* had existed back then, everyone in the cast would have had a Frenchie!

Frenchie popularity has ebbed and flowed but has

never gone away. We have always loved Frenchies and that's why they have popped up in films, so we can laugh at their antics and marvel at their wisdom. I loved that James Cameron took the trouble to include a shot of a Frenchie in his 1998 film *Titanic*. There was only one Frenchie on the ill-fated voyage and his name was Gamin de Pycombe, owned by First-Class passenger Robert Williams Daniel. In the film, the brindle Frenchie was seen walking (and doing his business) on the steerage class deck but Cameron cut the scenes of the dog struggling in the water after the ship sank (on 15 April 1912) in the final version because he felt it would be too upsetting. Sadly, in real life it seems the little Frenchie didn't survive the sinking: although an eyewitness said they saw him in the water, no one recorded his rescue.

But it isn't all doom and gloom for Frenchies. There are more than a dozen films in which Frenchies star, and most of them want to give those funny Frenchie features an airing. *Franky Goes to Hollywood* is a good laugh and if they ever do a sequel I'm happy to audition Eric. I think he'd walk the role – soft lad that he is!

The Frenchie is a dog for everyman – and I mean every woman too. We love them, and they can't fail to be loved. It must be that childlike quality or maybe it's just that they have a magical quality all of their own.

Chapter 3

A Clown in the Cloak of a Philosopher

Is a Frenchie right for me?

IN MY LIFE before Ern I was happy being a couch potato. Exercise had never really been one of my 'things' until I joined the cast of *TOWIE* and found myself on photoshoots with geezers who had abs like Spartacus. That was a real wake-up call to get up and off the couch, but if truth be told I still prefer to slob out than work out.

Although I didn't take the time to look into the personality of the Frenchie before I acquired Ern, I was relieved to discover that he was more than happy to accommodate and share my couch-potato habits. You only have to take one look at a Frenchie to know that they are not built for speed, agility or even long walks. Their wide and solid frame, barrel chest, flat nose and short legs can often get in the way of any kind of high-impact exercise and in rare bouts of speed they have all the athleticism of a small tank on manoeuvres.

The chunkiness of the breed is part of their charm. They look cuddly and, believe me, you know when you've been cuddled by a Frenchie. They size you up and they are focused because they absolutely need to show you affection. They properly demand it and they won't wait for an invitation to bustle up to you with a big smile on their face and be your friend. That's who they are, and I believe their big-heartedness is one of the reasons why, in 2017, they became one of the most popular breeds of dog in the UK, threatening to knock the Labrador and the pug off their pedestals. We like Frenchies because they love us.

Loyalty is a Frenchie speciality and although they are happy to share their love with your family and friends it's wise for any prospective Frenchie owner, especially singletons, to be aware that they can be a bit clingy. Ern loved me and because we only had each other I was the centre of his universe and focus of his absolute loyalty, a duty which he took very seriously – especially in the bedroom.

Believe me, it's not easy to maintain the air of romance when your devoted French bulldog is just the other side of the bedroom door. It's even more challenging when he whines as if he is being tortured, snuffles, snorts, sighs and generally grumbles out loud until he is allowed into the room. Frenchies never bark, unless they get excited and have tried all the other noises they can make, so I was spared that offering. Even so, my ever-faithful companion, Ern, had other ways of making his presence felt. Once in the room he would take up position by the bedside and start his staring and loud snuffling routine. If I could last out through all of that he would remain in position ready and waiting to wake me up by licking my toes!

I guess that's 'love me, love my dog' to the extreme but that was part of life with Ern. And it's now part of my life with Eric, who has dutifully taken over where Ern left off. Never a dull moment. That's another great thing about Frenchies. They are not only fiercely loyal and hell-bent on defending their family and home with their life, they also have a funny flip-side. They love a laugh and they are full of mischief. Perhaps that's why some people call them the clowns of the dog world? I can see it; after all they kind of wear their sense of humour on their sturdy exterior and that's probably a lot to do with their incredible ears.

They are called 'bat-like' ears and popping up on top of their flat-top, block-like heads the tall, rounded ears look as if they could have been borrowed from somebody else. I'll forgive people who think Frenchies look a bit odd – even though I think they look happy, smiley and I challenge anyone to not feel compelled to smile back when they meet one. But I can't accept criticism of those amazing ears. After all, it's those unmissable, trademark Frenchie lugs that set them apart from their cousins the bulldog and the pug.

When I finally read up on the history of Frenchies I liked the idea that they are rebels in the dog world. I respect individualism and the reason why Frenchies came to look the way they do today is, I think, fascinating, but sadly this 'look' doesn't come without their many associated health issues. And I respect the people, in the not-too-distant past, who believed in the breed and became so passionate about these little characters that they took on the establishment and critics and anyone else who tried so hard to make them conform to the 'norm'. I don't go with acceptance and never will. It's the people who have the integrity to stand up for what they believe in who bring about change and make a difference. And the Frenchie was and still is unique.

So … where was I?

When I was reading about the history of the Frenchie I noticed that the American Kennel Club classifies the breed as 'non-sporting' and says that they are bred as 'lapdogs'. I know what they mean but if you take that literally, believe me, there's no way you would want a Frenchie settled on your lap for any length of time. Well, not if you value having sensation in your legs. They are muscular power-packs.

Yes, they prefer to laze around and for a lot of people that's one of the lovely things about the breed, but when they're not lazing they love short walks and lots of play. As long as you're there leading the way, they'll follow you to the end of the earth. It's a bit like eating tapas: regular small portions work best. What they can't cope with is the heat. That flat nose means they can't get air into their lungs fast enough to cool down and in hot weather that can often pose a real danger of heatstroke. What's more, that scrunched-up nose is also the source of another common problem area for the Frenchie – flatulence.

I think Frenchie flatulence must be legendary. Well, I can tell you that it is in my home thanks to Ern and Eric. It's like most family secrets: it's rarely spoken about at family gatherings, but you can sense it's in the room. Vets will tell you that the reason they build up so much 'air' in their bodies is because short-faced breeds gulp air when they eat. And the air has to find its way out somehow. Just as it's good to know the biology of it all it's also good to be aware that this is the Frenchie's most silent and deadly weapon.

Ern was capable of epic bouts of flatulence and I'm convinced he chose his moments to release them for maximum effect. Ern was a perfect gentleman and always happy as long as I was around, but he wasn't so keen on competition and, in his mind, that included female company. He'd welcome anyone who came to visit and give them the old geezer greeting but when he thought the evening was going on a bit too long past his bedtime or things were getting a bit too intimate for his liking that's when he would release one of his famous gas bombs. The aroma would rise slowly from his fully stretched out form on the end of the sofa and then explode in your nostrils!

There's nothing quite like it for breaking the mood of a romantic moment or breaking the ice if things need a bit of jollying along in the conversation department because one of Ern's 'gas leaks' would always make people laugh – eventually. Now I wouldn't recommend this as a foolproof method of entertainment but imagine the performance of Ern and Eric together? I'm laughing about it now, but they really have sent people scattering, hands clasped to their faces.

Eric has taken up the mantle in this department with great enthusiasm and regularly clears the way in the local pubs and restaurants in which he is still allowed. The look he gives as he hears me say, 'Eric, what the hell was that?' is so innocent, as if butter wouldn't melt in his mouth, but to be honest I've sometimes been surprised that his efforts didn't strip paint off the walls. So be warned, it's part of the Frenchie make-up and something to get used to.

My mates on *TOWIE* will tell you that even if they love my dogs there have been times when the bum-wind problem has been so bad it has caused breaks in filming! And that's not a good thing when people are getting aggy in a scene and there's my dog stretching out on the floor, relaxing his body and releasing something silent but oh so deadly! It would usually be one of the girls who couldn't bear to work through it and the next thing I'd hear is: 'Pete, your dog has an evil arse – get him out of here!'

I would do the usual thing – rush in to grab the offender while everyone laughs their head off. If it was Eric, I'd have to wake him up before I could move him or, if he was totally zonked out, just pull him away from under everyone's noses.

Talking of bad habits, they have a few more that are worth mentioning to anyone thinking of taking one on because they come as part of the package. Snoring and wheezing are specialities and these dogs sleep a lot. Slobbering is another unfortunate Frenchie trait and I'd advise carrying a handkerchief to make sure you get to the goo before they plant it on you. A snail-trail of Frenchie saliva down your trousers is not a great look – I know because I've worn it out many times and sometimes it takes a long time for even your friends to say anything.

I'd say that smelly wind, snoring, wheezing and slobbering are probably the only not-so-good traits associated with Frenchies. The list of positives is a lot longer and for most people it probably starts with their looks because they are, I think, good-looking dogs. One thing people love about them is that their coats come in many colours. At least that's how it looks but they are all variations on three themes: brindle, fawn and pied (that's white with brindle patches). These are the breed standard colours and it's the brindle and fawn varieties we see the most – for instance, Ernest was a red-fawn and Eric a blue-fawn.

As a puppy Ern's coat was a very attractive burnt-orange colour with the darker brindle running through. I loved that puppy as soon as I saw him. He suited being 'red' because he was such a firecracker and so handsome and so, what I now know to be, 'classic' Frenchie. He was square, squat and had muscles like Popeye. He also developed a swagger that said: 'I'm not a bad-looking bloke!' And he was right.

Don't get me wrong, Ern wasn't arrogant. No, he was just a confident dog who had an air of 'I've arrived!' about him. This worked really well when we were filming together for *TOWIE* because Ern liked, or at least didn't mind, the cameras. As long as he could see me, he would sit quietly and show his good side for as long as we needed him to. He was very relaxed and happy to be a part of whatever happened to be going on.

You've heard of a horse of a different colour? Well, Eric was the dog version. When it comes to looks, he is without doubt a Frenchie, but he is not a classic Frenchie. For one thing Eric is smaller than Ern and slightly less muscular and although his coat is a beautiful blue-fawn (a grey with brindle undertones) he can appear a bit raggedy-around-the-edges (sorry Eric, glad you can't read this) compared to Ern's smooth, square lines. Ern was a tree-trunk of a dog and Eric more of a solid branch. Maybe put another way, it's the old Ray Winstone and Alan Carr thing again: if they were making a personal appearance Ern would be more like me and Ray in a white Tuxedo and black tie and Eric would be Alan in a bespoke pink lounge suit with an open collar. Smart but not the same.

Frenchies' coats are short and smooth, so they are very wash-and-go and low maintenance which, for many people, is a major plus-point when it comes to choosing a dog to suit their lifestyle, home and commitments. But don't think for one moment that your furniture, clothes and house guests will be hair-free because they won't. Frenchies are dogs after all, so those annoying little flyaway hairs will get everywhere ... just not in massive amounts. The challenge for any dog owner is to make sure the dog is still wearing more hair than they are.

The natural close crop also doesn't mean that they should skip a weekly bath – although a lot of Frenchies will dodge a dip if they have half a chance. Ern and Eric hate water, which has always made bath time more an event than just a routine part of pet care. I'd warn anyone reading this who is thinking of having a dog to remember this soggy-dog tip: clear the bathroom of anything you value and anything you want to keep dry. Oh, and prepare for trouble because Frenchies don't like water. As fast as I tried to cover Ern and Eric in water they shook it off – on me. So, it didn't take me long to work out that it was better for me and created less laundry if I stripped off and washed the dogs topless!

But it's not all about the mess of bath time with Frenchies; there's a serious side too. They aren't great swimmers. Their bodies are often far too chunky and their heads too heavy to keep them afloat, so if they fall in a pond, river, stream or swimming pool they won't usually be able to get out. When I say this I really know what I'm talking about because I nearly lost Eric this way.

Eric had not been with me long when we went to see a photographer friend to discuss my next calendar and, without thinking, I let Eric loose to have a run in the garden while I was chatting. Suddenly, I heard someone call over to say they had seen Eric by the fish pond. I ran as if the Devil was on my tail, and all I could think about was a news story I had read about the Hollywood actor, The Rock, who rescued his Frenchie, Brutus, from his swimming pool at home. The tiny pup had jumped in and sunk to the bottom head-first. I imagined the worst for Eric. Nightmare.

When I reached the pool I just jumped in and yanked Eric up and out by his harness. His face was a picture. I'm not sure what scared him the most: nearly drowning, me diving in all arms and legs to pull him out of the water or the size of the carp in the pool who looked big enough to swallow him whole! Funny now – but not at the time. I didn't see the danger ahead for Eric but I'm well aware of it now.

If you like a dog with a sense of humour, then look no further than the Frenchie. Not all the laughs are in that slightly Jack Dee expression – all furrowed brow, downcast eyes and air of misery. It's that underlying expression of 'I've got you worked out, mate' that should act as a warning to any owner who can't see or respect the Frenchie's sense of mischief.

Both Ern and Eric had 'Mischief' as their middle name and they could mug me off any time they liked, but, unlike with people, there's never a shred of malice in any of it. I'll give you a 'for instance': Eric loves to leave his scrunched-up plastic bottles (his favourite 'toys') and bones scattered just under the edge of the rug by the sofa. He knows I'll forget, tread on them and end up leaping around the room swearing and holding my injured foot in the air. I know he's not far away, having a good old grin!

And Ern? Well, for all his East End blokeiness he liked a smile at my expense from time to time. I know for a fact that when I'd be telling Nan how 'her Ern' was getting better at not jumping on the furniture and being a good lad and all that he would be getting ready to pounce on her sofa as soon as I left her house. When I looked back through the window he'd be sitting like a king on a throne! If I caught his eye he'd give me that look: 'Leave it out, Dad ... spare me the GBH on the ear'ole!'

Sometimes being with Ern and Eric when they were having a bit of fun with me was like being with Lockie and Arg on *TOWIE*. Harmless boy banter. But I needed to keep a step ahead with the dogs because, if your back was turned, they (well, Eric) would almost inevitably be up to something. Filming was mostly hazard-free when it was only me with Ernest because he liked to be right beside me and wasn't fazed by the cameras. But Eric, well, that was, and still is, a different experience. Even now, if you have anything less than 80 per cent attention on him while you're busy talking or even filming he will be up to something or he'll be looking for something to get up to.

I remember once, when we were filming one of the many intense one-to-one conversation pieces in the park, I had both dogs with me and on the lead so they could be close to me but out of shot. You see, it's OK to have them there but sometimes what the dogs are up to is a distraction for everyone taking part and, when it's shown, the viewer is distracted too. Everything was fine for a while and I was totally into the scene until, out of the corner of my eye, I saw Eric chomping on something. As I was talking I was trying to work out what it could be. Although I knew that if it had been anything dangerous someone would have stepped in and taken it off him, I still wanted to know what he was up to. I couldn't stop the take and risk naffing everyone off, especially as it was one of those deep, potentially emotional chats, so I decided to gradually reel in Eric's lead without anyone really noticing. I know what you're going to say ... it wasn't the brightest idea I've ever had but I think I would have got away with it if Eric had budged a single, solitary inch. As I started pulling on the lead he just became a solid, immovable, slobbering lump! It's like we were having a silent tug-of-war.

I'd say that was one of the longest takes I've known

on the show and how I kept my concentration I've no idea but as soon as the cameras stopped rolling I leant over to Eric, pulled him to me and looked him in the face – which was full of grass! Bits of grass were sticking out of his mouth at all angles. He looked like a country bumpkin chewing on not just one blade of grass but huge clumps at the same time. The rest of what he had 'enjoyed' had turned to green slop dripping from his lips. I think Eric was just bored! If he could speak he would have said: 'Dad, how long is this thing going to go on for because I've had enough now. What's next? Home to sleep? Lovely!' And here's me saying dogs don't judge or criticise. That's what he thought of my efforts on screen that day. Thanks, Eric, for putting me right on that one!

Frenchies are funny, clever, loyal, smart and everything their owners need them to be. At the same time, they are everything they want to be for themselves. They are free-thinkers and that's sometimes why their individuality can be mistaken for stubbornness. And it's why training must be consistent and send a clear message that you mean what you say, otherwise they will mug you off good and proper.

Now, dog training classes were not really Eric's thing. OK, I'll be honest … they were his thing but not for the right reason. He just liked meeting the other dogs, trying to make friends, stomping about a bit and not doing much work. It was a social outing for Eric and, while it was great to see him nudge and sniff the other 'trainees' until they got fed up of it and walked off, and although it was great for me to spend time with the lovely trainers, we weren't really getting anywhere. So we decided that it might be best if I was given all the techniques to try at home and that's what we did.

We're all motivated by something, food or money usually (peace of mind for me), and Frenchies will take food if it's offered. But these chunky guys can't risk being overweight because that will only add to their potential health problems. A bulkier body will only increase their snuffling and shortness of breath, as well as pressure on their joints, so better to use lots of praise and play to reward these guys. Reward them with their favourite ball and some fuss-time with you and they will love you even more for it.

These dogs are independent thinkers and strong characters. Eric loves me but he's a bit of a free spirit and he will show it in all sorts of ways. When we're having a night in, just us lads together, he will lie on top of me on the sofa and snore away for as long as I can stand it but if he decides it's bedtime he will take himself off – giving me a parting glance of: '… Well, you can stay up all night watching some crap film if you want to but to be honest ... I'm off to bed!' And that's what he does. He takes himself off to my bed and two seconds later the snoring begins again.

I'll admit I often miss the times with Ern when he was my shadow and only went to bed when I went to bed and never wanted to be in a different room to me, no matter what, but I admire Eric's independent ways. If he's never a danger to himself or anyone else, then he's fine and it's good to see him grow into his own person – or dog, I should say.

In our life after Ern I think Eric has grown as himself and to support me. He's still a bit of a doughnut, I'm happy to say, but now that he can't walk behind Ern any more we walk together and cast one shadow. And I find great strength in that. These dogs, honestly ... cute, funny, handsome and, inside each one, a core of steel.

I can get very emotional about Ern and Eric and that's from someone who was always very good at keeping my feelings hidden. It seemed safer to do that: the fewer feelings out there, the less chance of having them trodden on. Clearly my two Frenchies have changed all of that.

In one of the early episodes of *TOWIE*, Ern and I were introduced to a dog psychologist who 'read' Ern's feelings about me and, it appeared, Ern thought I wore my heart on my sleeve and was well up for getting hurt because of it. Emotions on my sleeve, eh? I guess I'd be better off keeping them in my pocket sometimes but when it comes to my dogs I can't help sharing the affection I have for them and reaching out to anyone who is thinking of inviting a Frenchie into their life, heart and home.

If you do your homework on Frenchies you will discover that they are very adaptable and happy in the town or the country. They have the smooth city look and, at the same time, a rustic appeal while their compact size, sturdy physique and basic laziness makes them the ideal dog for modern living.

It's worth remembering that other dogs don't always like Frenchies but that's a dog thing and perhaps to do with their flat face and big eyes. Other dogs may find these features harder to interpret so it switches on their fight-or-flight instinct. Very often Frenchies come off the worst as they loathe confrontation unless they are protecting their loved ones, in which case they won't take any agg and stand their ground.

Charming, loveable and adaptable, the Frenchie has just about smashed it as the ideal dog for singles, couples and families in the town or the country but, sadly, you can't escape the downside of their many potential health issues. As we've already seen, they can have problems breathing as well as suffering from spinal weakness, eye, joint and skin diseases. All of this can't be ignored because it can make their lives miserable and frequently adds up to some hefty vet bills. But mostly it's the heartache if a pet, any pet, falls ill and you see them suffering. The good news is that if your Frenchie escapes some of the well-known, more serious health problems, you could have them in your life for up to ten years – or maybe longer.

So, is there an ideal person for the Frenchie?

I can only answer for myself, Ern and Eric when I say that Frenchies are good for you. They are happy, playful dogs who have more games to offer up than Toys R Us! My Frenchies found the kid in me and gave me the OK to release my sensitive soul in a kind of rebirth. They thrive in a home where they are loved and included in what's going on. They are sociable and love to interact: shut them out and they will be miserable. I say, let them love you and be loved in return.

Chapter 4

Glitz, Glamour and Frenchies!

From the silver screen to the selfie scene

I'M A VERY lucky man. I have people in my life who love me, people who care what happens to me and who are there for me no matter what life and the consequences of stupid decisions throw at me. And, if I look back at how my career has panned out so far and how I've handled opportunities that have come my way, I believe I've had luck on my side – part-time, at least.

When I was offered the chance to appear in ITVBe's *TOWIE*, I think Lady Luck was standing at my side giving me a good shove in the right direction. After all, I had been putting messages out to the universe for a while, hoping somebody was listening to my call-out for something new to happen or a fresh challenge to come my way. I had been throwing all kinds of ideas around and thinking about all kinds of ventures. And there it was. I hadn't seen myself as a reality TV personality, but I knew Ernest would be perfect for the role. And if he could do it, then I'd have to give it a go too.

I remember saying to the production team that with me it would always be a case of 'love me, love my dog' and I'll always be grateful that they understood where I was coming from. When I signed up I knew that it wouldn't always be possible to include Ern in every episode with me, but it was enough that we were accepted as a 'package' for the show. We were in this together and I liked that.

Although I was introduced as a new cast member for the Marbs vacation that summer of 2015, as I mentioned before, I made my first proper *The Only Way Is Essex* appearance with Ernest taking a walk in the park to meet cast members Jess, her little Yorkshire terrior Bella, and her Nanny Pat. With every step we took towards the meet-up point I had a good feeling. A feeling that this was the perfect way to start this new chapter in my life. I loved meeting Nanny Pat for the first time. What a great lady Nanny Pat Brooker was. And it felt right to introduce me and Ern to the programme that way, the two of us walking in the park – something we have repeated many times in the programme since. I was sure that Ern would be an instant hit, not just with Jess's dog and the rest of the human cast but with the viewers too!

Ern didn't have to do anything special, just being Ern was special enough. We looked like a couple of geezers doing our usual slow strut through the park. Ern looked every inch the man-dog and very polished with his red-fawn coat shining and a lovely deep orange colour. We were in our smart casual gear that day and I was so proud of him. This was it – it all felt right and like the beginning of something that we could enjoy together.

So, picture the scene: big bruiser Ernest stomps up to tiny Bella to make friends, but for some reason the whole thing ends up with Ern running away from the little Yorkie! What the hell happened? I'm not sure, but Ern was so terrified he ran and nearly fell into the lake!

It was unusual for Ern to leave me feeling a bit embarrassed but that day I couldn't help it. I think everyone put it down to first day nerves, which was really generous of them, but I was seriously hoping it wouldn't happen again!

I remember my mum saying that when you start something new and you're digging inside yourself for confidence, always remember your roots and how proud you are to be an Essex boy. Family roots are important to me and I know Mum's concern was that I would get carried away with the glitz and glamour. I was already a party-boy, remember, so I'm guessing she feared that I would get carried away and the extra partying would all go to my head – and not in a good way. I wouldn't be surprised if my family were looking to Ernest to keep me on the straight and narrow!

Don't get me wrong, I'm not going to pretend that I wasn't attracted by some of the showbiz stardust. Who doesn't like hanging out with their mates and getting the chance to party and show off in a new whistle (that's cockney for suit) on a regular basis? That was something I had always enjoyed in my spare time so how amazing was it to do that for the day job? I had a reputation for my sharp suits and had always put a lot of thought into buying each one, which was probably one of the reasons why that look became my signature for a long time. But this was a 'new' me and with the new job came a new handle – Pete, the Essex Pirate.

OK, I get it: the beard, the tatts and the long hair. I wasn't going to swap Ern for a parrot on my shoulder any day soon but social media Pete 'the Pirate' Wicks seems here to stay. And I've grown used to him now, this bloke with his addiction to tattoos and the hair, once very short, now long and more comfortable and more the person I am. *TOWIE* certainly opened the social media floodgates for me and Ernest and then, when Eric joined us, the Wolfpack took on an energy all of its own. Ern and Eric were the stars and I've been happy to keep supplying the photos and the news updates ever since. It has been so incredible to be a part of the whole social media whirl that has swept us up and for that I want to

...he Wolfpack. Ern always took the lead, my alpha. Eric happily running along like the little doughnut he is.

Frenchies sleep … a lot! Ern and Eric would happily snore their way through an evening.

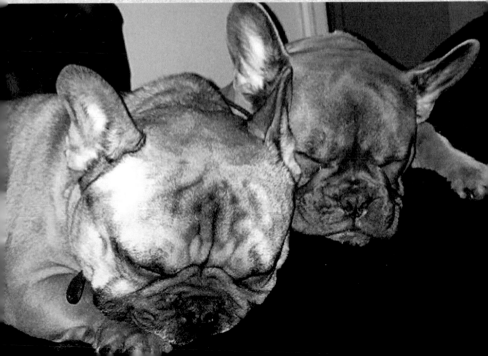

Ern was my world. A beautiful red-fawn French Bulldog, he was a proper geezer, named after my Uncle Ernest.

t was lovely to have Ern sleeping on my chest at night, being my adoring shadow and my boy.

He was always posing for the camera. He had a natural stage presence and knew how to show his best side. He was an instant *TOWIE* hit.

I had the happiest times with Ern and Eric. We were the Wolfpack and we did everything together.

When you see the boys standing together, Eric is an ever-so-much-slighter version of the mighty and robust Ernest.

Frenchies love getting comfy, and Eric and Ern would always jump up on the sofa with me, stretching out until they had most of the room!

couldn't have chosen better names for Eric and Ern – look at these two little comedians.

Frenchies can be a *bit* clingy. I never got a moment's peace with these two around. They'd follow me everywhere – even to the bathroom.

Like all French Bulldogs, Eric loves short walks and lots of play.

With his not-so-square head, narrower shoulders and longer back, Eric is a variation on the Frenchie theme – his genetic make-up got shaken up somewhere along the line.

Look how cute Eric was when I first locked eyes on him. After everything he'd been through, he was still so trusting and loyal.

Eric taking a break on a photoshoot. Although he's not *quite* as professional as Ern was, all the cast and crew still love him.

French Bulldogs are the ultimate companion dogs – here we are on the way back from a meeting in London.

Although you must give your Frenchie a regular check-over for health problems, this is NOT what I mean when I recommend a 'man maintenance' routine …

thank our thousands of followers from the bottom of my heart. And of course, to thank the Frenchies at the centre of my universe – Ern and Eric.

I'm pleased that the boys can never let this popularity go to their silky, shiny heads. They are oblivious to the number of adoring fans they have following them and, if you're a dog, I suspect that's the best way to be. Eric's brother, Guzzy, is also a social media sensation: just more proof, if proof were needed, that Frenchie good looks run in the family. I know they are good-looking boys and I'm so proud of them and always like to show them off but there's no way I would describe them as celebrity dogs. To me, what's more important than anything is that they are my day-to-day companions. But a Frenchie owned by an international sporting hero, Hollywood star or pop icon is a dog with incredible power.

From the second that football legend David Beckham received Coco the Frenchie as a present from his wife, Victoria, social media buzzed, and the popularity of the breed zoomed astronomically. When they added puppy Scarlet to the family more folk clamoured to get their hands on one of the little dogs owned by the famous Beckhams. These Frenchies were in the spotlight, which was shared by the pets of other lovers of the breed such as Hollywood actors Hugh Jackman, Reese Witherspoon,

Keanu Reeves and the late Carrie Fisher, who took her dog, Gary, everywhere with her. Lovely, faithful Gary, with his trademark stick-out tongue, was with Carrie on the flight out of London in December 2016 when she was taken ill and then, sadly, passed away in hospital four days later. Gary was with her the whole time. The actress said she and Gary were inseparable and they were to the end. I totally empathise with Carrie and, I guess, with Gary too. He would have grieved for her the way I have grieved for Ern. The poor little guy.

With 141,000 followers on Instagram, Gary is one of many influential Frenchies who have captured hearts the world over. When an image of Gary watching his late mum in her final *Star Wars* appearance as the iconic Princess Leia, in *The Last Jedi* (2017), was posted on Instagram, his thousands of followers felt Gary's pain. He was not only Carrie Fisher's self-appointed therapy dog and her constant companion, through the power of social media Gary also became a friend to thousands.

Tabloid headlines, gossip magazine photo spreads, front-page news and the reach of Instagram, Twitter and Facebook keep the Frenchies of the rich and famous in our faces. Queens of Pop Lady Gaga and Madonna are never shy of showing off their Frenchie friends, and British television personalities like chat show host

Jonathan Ross and fashion guru Gok Wan show the adaptable nature of this lovely breed and how they can easily fit into many different lifestyles, even the often hectic lives of those involved in the media and showbiz worlds. All these lovely Frenchie people reaching into the hearts and minds of their followers is a wonderful thing and it's great that they can do it all through the massive reach of social media.

It doesn't matter if we think that social media is a blessing or the work of the Devil, we all know that, right now, it's the most powerful method of communication available to all of us. It has its upsides and downsides, for sure, but for Frenchie owners who want to share the love they have for their own dogs, as I do, it's now part of our everyday lives. We can all view the lifestyle of the stars and follow the antics of their Frenchies. And we love doing it, probably making a ritual of it. We can see the dogs enjoying a celebrity lifestyle – loved and cared for, and provided with the best of everything. And that's where the danger lies: people want that glamorous life themselves and superficially it can seem like you need to have the dogs to get that look. Maybe they think the lifestyle goes with the dog: get the dog, get the lifestyle? You'd hope no one would make that mistake but part of you also knows that's exactly how it works for some.

Frenchies are popular because they are the choice of many celebrities and this is one of the reasons why the demand for the puppies is outweighing the supply. If registered breeders can't keep up with the supply, then puppy farms and illegal trafficking from Eastern Europe will fill the gap. It's not right. Nothing about it is right but it is happening. People want the dogs because, right now, they are the celebrity's choice but that doesn't make them the right choice for everyone. And what happens when it all goes wrong?

Who would believe that people would give up their dogs for reasons like: 'he didn't match the furniture', 'she was too friendly towards other dogs and people on walks', 'I won a holiday and couldn't take him with me', 'he didn't like it when we played dress-up', 'he pants too much' … and so it goes on. It makes me so angry to read these excuses from poor excuses for human beings. They are all the more shocking because they are all true responses from a survey held before last Christmas (2017). You would think that people would be ashamed to admit such things, but they are not. It's all about getting dogs for all the wrong reasons.

Without wanting to sound like some kind of dour preacherman, I think it's fair to say, in the spirit of the mixed bag of people who've said a version of these words before, 'With great power there must also come great responsibility.' It's a big call out to people who have a platform to use their voice to do good for dogs.

I know, I'm on my soapbox again, givin' it agg, but I absolutely believe that dog lovers, especially those with celebrity status and social media profile, should make use of their privileged position and stand up for what they believe in. Every responsible pet owner can be a voice for the animals and can make a difference. If that means encouraging people to do their homework before they get a dog, or help an animal charity as a volunteer or look further afield and support a dog charity overseas then I'll be happy. Helping to rehabilitate rescue dogs like Eric must be very rewarding and to be part of that dog's next stage in life is an honour. Maybe the next step means a second chance at a forever home. People might stumble, but they should be supported to persevere and work through it. You don't give up on a dog because it's a bit broken. We're all a bit broken inside.

TOWIE has been good to me and through my time on the show so far I've met some amazing people, including hard-working celebrities who are putting some serious action behind their words and their social media posts. They say action speaks louder than words and these guys really live up to that and I wish I could name them all here. I hope that when I've met these folk at animal welfare events at the Houses of Parliament and at the Animal Hero Awards and other events highlighting the work of special organisations and incredible individuals, I've made it clear how much I admire them. Speaking out is not something they have to do; they choose to do it. It's always easier to do nothing or be an armchair critic but the people I'm talking about get off their backsides and go where they need to be to save the lives of animals and raise awareness of their suffering. They are using their celebrity platform to make a difference for animals. I aspire to follow in their footsteps ... and day by day, I'm getting there.

I'm saying that 'I'm getting there' because I think we are all a work in progress. We are all working towards being the best we can be and if we are dog lovers and owners, then our dogs take that journey with us and that can make it even more interesting.

When Eric joined the cast of *TOWIE* he didn't go for the usual calm, professional entrance that everyone had been used to with Ernest. Eric preferred his own version, which on that day went something like this: 'Hmm, I know, while Dad's involved in a conversation I'll just roll in this dog poo and see what happens next.' I can see

Ern's face looking at Eric now – if dogs could roll their eyes he would have done – as someone asked: 'What the hell is he doing?' Sadly, I knew exactly what he was doing and as he rolled and rolled some more I just hoped that my colleagues sharing the scene would be able to put up with the stink rising from my dog while we finished the filming. I'm not sure how we got all that done without collapsing in fits of laughter. Probably thanks to a patient camera crew and my good friends.

On that occasion I think Ern would have preferred the earth to open up and swallow Eric before he could do anything else to embarrass the Wolfpack. But it was only the start of little Eric's antics on and off screen.

In his early days on *TOWIE* Eric didn't seem to have much respect for the world of showbiz. He is probably at his most frustrated on photoshoots and, as I mentioned earlier, he made that perfectly obvious from his first assignment when he fell asleep waiting for his turn in front of the camera. This has become his habit in every photoshoot ever since. Perhaps he's a narcoleptic or something but he just can't stay awake!

When Ernest was alive I could tell that he disapproved of Eric's sleeping habits. Ern's professionalism shone through every time a camera was pointed in his general direction. He was able to switch into 'actor mode' at the drop of a hat and a permanent feature of Ern's time on *TOWIE* was his talent for shadowing me. He would only ever share the spotlight – never hog it. As a human he would have made a fine actor and been a real gentleman on set. That's probably why Eric's antics annoyed the hell out of him. There would be Ern, budding thespian, looking disapprovingly at Eric, all impatient and sleepy. I can see the look on his face now and if he could speak he'd have probably said the same as me: 'Eric, you're such a doughnut. But you're my doughnut.'

As we are in the world of 'lights, camera, action!', I sometimes worry about Eric and his reluctance to face the limelight. If you are lucky enough to have Eric awake, then he's a great guy and you'll be guaranteed some laughs along the way, but you can tell that if he were a human he would not have chosen reality TV as a career. I've told you he would have made a great taxi driver: lovely and chatty and loving people all the time on a one-to-one basis ... but put him in a social gathering with a load of people and he's not such a happy bunny. He'll do the walking in the park thing but anything where the attention is on him and he will try to disappear up my armpit and pretend he's invisible.

Camera-shy Eric has often put me in an embarrassing spot filming for *TOWIE* but *any* occasion where he finds himself the centre of attention is an invitation for Eric to cause mayhem, even when he's not sleepy. The photoshoot for the front cover of this book was one prime example of Eric not playing ball, and me ending up looking a right doughnut. Rattling keys, saying his name in baby-talk, slapping the photographer on the head … I tried anything and everything to get Eric to look at the camera, but I failed! The only time he sat still enough to take a shot was when he sat down to lick his own nuts.

Talk about never working with children or animals!

I wonder if dogs can suffer from body dysmorphia. Is that possible? Maybe he is conscious of his wonky teeth and that makes him camera shy. I've had my teeth done so maybe I should do the same for Eric? Don't worry, I'm only joking; I'm sure he's fine but he is painfully shy compared to Ern, who would lap up the attention whenever it came his way.

Ern had a purpose in life and that was to look after Eric and me. Without our guardian angel now we must look after each other – with a bit missing. It's a bit like driving along and a wheel comes off your car: you'll carry on moving for a while but you're aware there's something not quite right. But we're doing it and I think if Ern is watching us from a higher place somewhere then he will be happy that we are getting there.

I used to tell Ern everything and now it's Eric who gets all the angst and it's a great release for me that I can do that. The relief is that Eric, as with all dogs, never judges me, so whatever I share with him he never leaves me feeling like a complete tit. But I'm careful and considerate to his needs because I can feel him picking up on my energy and it's not fair to expect too much of him. I'm especially aware of this with Eric because he is missing Ern too. I don't want to be the idiot who brings him down as he's the geezer with the power to laugh and make me laugh too.

I've already told you that if Eric had middle names, 'Mischief' would be one of them, but 'Chaos' would be the other. Chaos, because that's what follows him wherever he goes. When the TOWIE cast decided to organise a fundraising event to benefit the local dog re-homing centre, the winning idea was a fancy dress photoshoot which was a competition to find the dog and owner who looked most like each other. For me there was only one costume that would work: we would be Pirate Pete and Eric his faithful sea dog!

I had eyepatches and bandanas for both of us, with a pirate's hook up my sleeve for good measure. We had lots of fun that day, probably one of my favourite days filming with all the dogs, and I really thought we looked the best dog-and-owner combo. But, we didn't win. To put Eric out of his costume-wearing misery I set about taking off his bandana, which he didn't mind at all, but as I went for his eyepatch he tore off around the room with me in hot pursuit! How could I have known that he would like to wear an eyepatch? I didn't catch him for the rest of the day, so the eyepatch stayed on!

I like to think that we are there for each other and amidst the glitzy moments of our working career we still have all the emotional bonding that existed in our life with Ern. I am always there for him and Eric is certainly always there for me. We live in a home that partly reflects the TV life, but some people might call it a bit of a shrine to Ern. I'd prefer to call it a dog lover's home where photographs of my Frenchies are on show and I have Frenchie sculptures to add to the mix in my man cave. The front garden is enclosed for Frenchie safety and there are toys and treats around to remind any visitor that this is the home of a man who loves his dogs. Simple.

TOWIE turned my life upside down, not in a bad way, only that I had to open myself up to whatever happened as the journey progressed. That can mean you're on a pedestal one minute and on the ground the next. As someone who doesn't show emotion easily I found it to be an experience that tested me, and could leave a not-so-strong person feeling exposed and raw. I've always considered myself lucky that I've had my dogs to come home to and someone to tell my troubles to. The Wolfpack was my security and comfort blanket and the one thing in my life that I knew would never let me down.

When Ernest died I had Eric and my family and friends for support, but his death was a catalyst for taking a good look at my life and stripping it back to the real Pete Wicks. I thank my Frenchies for this because dogs are the greatest levellers. At the end of the day, no matter how much glitz and glamour you have in your life, dogs will always remind you of what's real and that's what I needed more than anything when Ern was gone.

I looked in the mirror and what did I see? As I said earlier, the ink on my body tells a story all of its own, so I started there. I've already told you how my nan's love of American Indian culture found its way into my tattoo history, but all the symbolism of the culture that appears all over my body didn't begin and end with that one sketch of a warrior. Any lover of tatts will tell you they can get addictive and you can want to collect them for all kinds of reasons or sometimes no particular reason at all. And then there are the ones you go for on the spur of the moment – otherwise known as mistakes. Like the 'four-leaf' clover that I asked for in a tattoo parlour in Ireland. I was there with a bunch of mates who didn't foresee the potential problem. I wanted a four-leaf clover for good luck. What I got was a three-leaf shamrock, but I didn't notice that until I got home! My mum told me that the three-leaf shamrock is connected to Ireland's St Patrick, who adopted the shamrock to represent the Holy Trinity (Father, Son and Holy Ghost) so no wonder that's what I got. Perhaps I was being taught a history lesson by my tattooist, which was a bit wasted on me because the only thing I learnt from that experience was never to have a tatt when you're drunk!

I say that and then I look at the figure with the foot that looks spookily like a penis and the Latin quote that remains a mystery to me today. I hate to think I was mugged off but it's a bit late to cry over spilt ink!

Eagle, wolf, tiger, hummingbirds, dragonflies and ... butterflies. Animals have always been a feature of my life so it makes sense they appear in the story on my skin. I have over twenty butterflies scattered around, and all are different in size and colour. I love them because they symbolise transition. I believe that we are all in a state of change all the time, trying to find out who we are and where we are meant to be.

The outward image we project can give a picture of where we are financially, emotionally and physically and signals how we want others to see us. It's part of how we want to be accepted by others and displays our status in society. Some people make their dogs part of their own created image, an image they want others to see where the dog is nothing more than an accessory. But dogs are so much more than that. And ironically, they themselves don't give a damn about how we look. We only have to be exactly who we are for them. It's human beings who make things difficult, who play games and want to outdo each other – never dogs. Dogs are honest. The only problem with their honesty is that they can't hide fear, which often shows itself as aggression. That's one of the many reasons why I feel for rescue dogs; they don't know what's happened to them to make them feel that way. They don't understand what triggers that reaction within themselves. We humans have a lot to answer for in so many ways.

My butterfly tattoos symbolise journeys in life that may not always go to plan, or that may sometimes go completely wrong. But they take us to the person that we want to be and that's why we can't make room for regret. Regret is the worst feeling of all and to guard against it we can't allow ourselves to be stopped by others on our journey. I believe we are all looking to be the best version of the person we are. I'm not there yet. I'm still on my journey so will keep adding to my butterflies to symbolise transition and the hummingbirds who symbolise eternal devotion. These little birds are some of the most beautiful creatures on the planet and were venerated by the Aztecs for their energy and potency. But they are also ferocious fighters always ready to defend their territory – if they have to. These hummingbirds are added to the dragonflies that represent change and self-realisation. The kind that comes of emotional maturity and understanding of a deeper meaning of life.

My journey is to find peace with myself – to feel as good on the inside as the butterfly looks on the outside in its final incarnation. Then I'll know that I've reached who I'm supposed to be.

Finding out who we are is up to us. We all have a vision of ourselves and how we want to be seen by other people. I think we know when we get there, and we can then be happy that we have reached the end of our journey.

But one thing I know is that sometimes, as part of our journey, we have to face up to things that are difficult, so I knew it was my duty to find out more about the darker side of the Frenchie breed's popularity ...

Chapter 5

Trouble in Store

The dark side of pedigree puppies

WHEN I WAS first introduced to Eric at the rescue centre I didn't know the first thing about puppy trafficking or any of the issues surrounding pedigree dogs being imported into the UK. Hearing my pup's story and how he would have suffered in the first weeks of his life on a puppy farm somewhere in Hungary was almost too much to bear. I imagined his mum still there, caged and condemned to a life sentence of torture as a breeding machine and I wanted to go out and grab hold of the people responsible along with the officials who, it seems to me, are allowing this cruel trade to continue. I couldn't get it out of my head that this is how we are treating man's best friend – for money. What an unbelievable betrayal of a dog's trust.

I needed to know more.

In my opinion, when money is someone's main motivator then they are capable of anything and cruelty becomes a quick way to get the job done and get the cash in their hands. Puppy smuggling is a multi-million-pound industry with layers of interested parties from the cesspit dwellers at the bottom of the pile who acquire the multiples of pedigree breeding bitches to start the sorry business, to the poor excuses for human beings who are the puppy 'farmers', dealers, transporters and sellers. There is corruption (and exchange of cash) at every level. My nan always said that the love of money is the root of all kinds of evil and I now know that dog trafficking is one of the evils that is thriving in our world today. The most frustrating thing about it is that it's happening right in front of us, but we can't see it.

Some of the puppies who end up on display for sale in pet shops, online websites or sold from private addresses could have found their way there from either legal or illegal puppy farms in the UK or overseas. Any pup that is being sold in an environment where you don't get to see them interacting with their mum and away from its place of birth is likely to be sold by a third-party seller (not the breeder) and a victim of irresponsible breeding.

Nowadays so many pups are being brought in illegally from Eastern Europe and the numbers appear to be growing. Sticking to figures for a minute, some animal organisations claim that over a quarter of a million dogs travelled to Britain in 2016, which is three times more than in 2011. To me that increase is horrific! It's totally out of order, especially when you hear how the dogs are kept before they even start their journey to be sold.

If you can bear to watch any of the footage captured

by dog welfare teams acting undercover on legal or illegal puppy farms you will see the filthy conditions that the bitches and pups are forced to live in. Hidden in basements or outbuildings, stacked in jagged, rusty metal cages, the breeding bitches are kept in the cold and dark. They have little food and only have access to water when it's given. They are not exercised so their muscles waste away, many have ear infections and have rotten teeth, and all show signs of malnourishment and ... fear. Some breeding dogs are virtually hairless due to stress or skin disorders and it's not unusual to see them struggle with respiratory problems caused by the conditions they are living in. There is no veterinary care and no escape. This is a prison and they are condemned to a life sentence.

Even for those breeding dogs who are rescued when their farm is exposed by the authorities or an investigating charity, the difficulties don't end there. Ten years in near solitary confinement without care or compassion leaves a dog with scars, both physically and of course emotionally. When the only human contact you've ever known is the person who reaches into your cage to take your pups away, being cradled in the hands of a rescuer must seem traumatic at first.

Fear is a massive controller and these poor mums live in fear every day. It's all they know. It's heartbreaking to watch them wince and blink when they are brought out of their dark prison and into the daylight, sometimes for the first time in their entire lives. Some are unrecognisable as specific 'breeds' because they have lost their fur to skin mite infestations or their bodies have been distorted by disease or an injury they have been forced to live with. The physical and mental damage these breeding dogs suffer at the hands of their captors is criminal. And it *is* a genuine crime to breed puppies on farms this way. The more I delved into the whole sorry saga of puppy smuggling, the more I felt sick. But I couldn't look away or stop asking questions. Turning your back on something doesn't mean it has gone away. It just makes you another person who pretends it's not happening.

The big question is: why are the puppies being trafficked?

And the answer is? Well, quite simply, because they can be. Shockingly, the third-party route to market for smuggled pups is legal in the UK and actually encourages pups to be imported whether legally or illegally. There's no concern for the breed or the puppies' welfare when they are sold via third parties, without their mum and away from where they were born. Also, there is a demand for so-called cheap designer breeds in the UK. Pugs, chow-chows, Chihuahuas, dachshunds and, yes … Frenchies.

Because ethical, responsible and accountable breeders with high welfare standards in the UK are always undercut by low-welfare, battery-farmed pups, it's obvious these third-party sellers can make a quick buck. It's a year-round trade for the bad guys, but in the lead-up to Christmas things get worse as the demand for these cheap, unethically bred puppies goes through the roof. Thousands of puppies will change hands for tens of thousands of pounds.

Some animal welfare organisations highlighted the horrors of smuggling in 2014, which was two years after the government relaxed the Pet Travel Scheme. And that must be more than a coincidence. It's easy to see how owners must have thought the pet passport was a really good idea, especially people who wanted to take their dog on European holidays with them. But relaxing the scheme for some gave others with a more sinister motive the loopholes they needed. They could now move dogs between countries easily, simply by using false documentation. The change played right into the smugglers' hands.

Eventually the flood of illegally trafficked puppies from Eastern Europe was noticed by dog charities and other animal welfare bodies. They discovered that many of the puppies making the journey were popular cheap pedigree breeds in high demand in the UK. They were mostly underage, unvaccinated and most importantly without their mothers. But it's still going on, and in even higher numbers. Everything about this trade is wrong and, most chilling of all, it's done without a shred of thought for the welfare of the dogs. The puppies and their mums are just objects to be cruelly traded. To the smugglers they are not living, breathing creatures; they are money on four legs. And if you doubt that for a single second, you only need to hear that some of the pups have had their tails cut (docked) and their ears clipped roughly by hand with scissors. There's no anaesthetic, and only vodka for an antiseptic. Many of them have scratches and untreated wounds just because of how and where they have been kept and it's not unusual for litters of pups to have problems with their skin, eyes and ears. Most likely their mums have the same problems and will have to carry on suffering behind closed doors, and so will the many litters of pups that come after.

If the smuggled pups are lucky enough to have survived the journey and be offloaded and passed into the care of local rescue shelters they will be seen by a vet for the first time in their lives. But until then, no one really knows where they have come from. They have no medical or family history. No clue if they have any genetic problems or serious illnesses ... and they are all headed for the UK's unsuspecting puppy buyers.

I was told that one in every ten puppies smuggled into the country doesn't survive. And when you hear all they have suffered from birth, the only surprise is that any of them survive at all. The little ones must be so stressed on the journey, and it doesn't get any better for them when they arrive in the UK. If they're not discovered when their transportation reaches the border control at Dover or Folkestone they will travel on until they reach the third-party dealers, legal or illegal: it's through these sellers that the smuggled puppies pop up for sale to the public.

Now I don't want to sound as if I'm preaching on the subject and I don't want to go pointing any fingers at people who are looking for a Frenchie puppy (or any of the other so-called designer breeds). After all, I decided I wanted a Frenchie and went looking for one, and I found Ernest. But my later journey to find Ern's companion took me down a different road. My visits to my local rescue centre introduced me to a whole new world of rescue dogs – and not just the sadly unwanted crossbreeds, but pedigree puppies, and lots of them. If Eric and his mates hadn't been taken in by the shelter they would have ended up in the hands of third-party sellers and offered for sale in licensed pet shops, garden centres, home-based sellers or, dodgiest of all, sold anonymously online and handed over out of the back of a van in a car park or a layby. These 'man in a van' sales have a lot to answer for. The puppy will be cheaper, by a long chalk. You are getting a bargain puppy because they have a lot of puppies to shift and they don't want the cost of feeding them. There's pressure on to get rid of them before the pups grow out of their tiny, cute and adorable stage. They are bargain puppies for a reason – they have a sell-by date.

This is in no way a dig at dog lovers looking for their perfect puppy, because the public will always try to buy the dogs in good faith. They won't see the mum, or know if the puppy they are looking at has any genetic conditions or any of the hidden health problems linked to being raised on a filthy puppy farm. But it stands to reason that unhealthy conditions are likely to produce unhealthy pups. Also, there are no papers and no way of tracing anything back through the seller so there's no breeder accountability. And that's also true of legal and illegal puppy farms closer to home; in Wales and the Republic of Ireland the farms are producing the majority of irresponsibly-bred pups for Great Britain. For example, after being smuggled out of the republic by boat they land in Scotland and are passed on to third-party dealers. The puppies' mothers are back in Ireland, nowhere in sight.

If I ever met the people who put Eric, his mum and his brothers and sisters through all of this, I know that I'd totally lose it. But I also know that just losing my temper wouldn't get me anywhere. Talking to the right people could make a difference. Taking action is the only thing that will raise awareness about the trade in puppies and get people to ask questions before they buy. The thing is, getting to the source of the problem of dog trafficking and everything associated with it is a bit like trying to unravel a heap of spaghetti: it's a hidden trade (until the pups reach the sellers and dealers) and it's difficult to police. And with budget cuts and a shortage of border control staff the smugglers seem to have the situation weighted on their side, so tackling this problem at the border is unlikely to work.

I'm discovering that the pet industry, together with its corporate partners, is a very complicated beast but I'm also seeing, with a lot of help from my newfound friends who dedicate their lives and skills to improving animal welfare, that there is a simple way to look at it: if every puppy comes from an 'accountable breeder' who can be open and transparent about the background and family history of their breeding bitches, stud dogs and their pups, then we would see an end to third-party sellers and the shady dealings that produce unhealthy and unhappy pups. Cracking down on the third-party sellers would end the chain the illegal smugglers and legal dealers and pet shops use to make their money. This ban would also be easy to enforce and make the situation much clearer for people buying a puppy, greatly helping to protect the welfare of the dogs too.

Is that solution too simple?

In my search for more information on puppy smuggling and Eric's journey to the UK, I have met some incredible people who are doing amazing things to improve the future of animal welfare in the UK. One of the organisations I came across on my voyage of discovery is Pup Aid which is a national awareness campaign both highlighting the horrors of puppy farming and promoting rescue pet adoption. Since adopting Eric I've been to a number of national events where people who really care about animals gather to share ideas and, well, educate people like me. I don't mind that one bit because that's exactly what I want – to know more. When I met the TV vet, Marc Abraham, and heard why he founded Pup Aid in 2009 I could see that he was someone who could back up his own chat.

One of the first times I met Marc the vet we were at an animal welfare event at the House of Commons and I can tell you that this man is relentless when it comes to lobbying in Parliament. I recognise the terrier instinct in him and thanks to Marc and his colleagues – who are not afraid to say what needs to be said to Members of

Parliament – the dirty subject of puppy farming is a hot topic in Westminster. As a practising vet, Marc sees what can happen to the puppies bred on puppy farms, as they can often fall ill not long after finding their forever home, and he sees the distress this causes their owners. All they did was buy the puppy they wanted, never expecting to spend so much time and money with their vet. There are so many stories that end like this and they are so upsetting. Hearing them is not good for my peace of mind, especially when I know they are all true.

What can we do to help?

We can use our people power and lean on our MPs to influence change and drive legislation to ban third-party sellers through. The decision-makers are finally starting to sit up and take notice but bringing about change can be a long and frustrating process, and the traffickers are always finding new ways to work the system and deceive buyers. They think nothing of faking Kennel Club pedigree certificates; it's the norm for puppy farmers who are operating both legally and illegally. They probably have a nothing-to-lose attitude although the maximum sentence for animal cruelty has recently been increased to five years.

A reputable breeder will always want a good, safe home for their pups, so they won't rush you into a decision – you may even have to go on a waiting list for a pup. And that's worth it when you know you will have a heathy pup at the end of it all. They will make sure you always see the pups interacting with their mum in the place they were born, will ask you lots of questions and expect you to ask plenty too, and they will never meet you at a random location to hand the puppy over. It's worth taking the time to check out if the breeder is recommended by the Kennel Club (KC) Assured Breeder Scheme so you know that you are talking to the real deal not a bootlegger. If they don't check out as KC Assured then do yourself and the pups a favour by acting on your suspicions. Report any shifty or shady behaviour to the police, Trading Standards, local authorities or the RSPCA to investigate.

This is big business for a lot of bad people with no thought for animal welfare, and they are getting harder to catch. Trying to pin them down is like nailing jelly to a wall and all the time they are adding new levels of cruelty, but the good news is that they can and are being caught. Pups sold by third parties will rarely be vaccinated, microchipped or be accompanied by legitimate paperwork. All this happens in the shadows, but if no one buys from a third party – that's puppy dealers, pet shops, garden centres and other outlets where you don't see their mum or the place they were born – then the demand will, eventually, drop away.

Puppies trafficked into the UK are all a mother's offspring. They have often been deprived of their mother's milk and love and turned into an object for sale. To legal and illegal dealers the puppies are just cash on four legs and not living creatures with needs and feelings at all. They travel thousands of miles in dreadful conditions at just a few weeks old with not even the basic comforts of food, water and warmth. It kills me to even imagine the pain and the fear they must feel, and that's only if they are not drugged to the eyeballs to keep them quiet. The dogs don't have a voice – but we do. That's why knowing about puppy smuggling and the third-party trade is so important but doing something to bring it to an end and protect dogs like Eric is vital.

Eric was one of the lucky ones – he was not obviously psychologically scarred by his experiences as he was rescued early and the dog shelter did such splendid work rehabilitating him. In fact, knowing what I know now about Eric's background on a puppy farm in Hungary I find it extraordinary that his affectionate nature is so undimmed. I wonder if dogs feel that massive sensation of relief that we sometimes get when we know that we've made it and we're home and safe. If they do feel that warm rush of 'ahhhh' then Eric will know it well. His time in rescue would have been his first experience of kindness, the first hands to show him care and love. Kind voices to encourage him to eat and a warm lap to sleep on. No cages, no bars and no cold concrete to lie on. Instead, there were beds and blankets and bowls of food and water. And then came me.

In our Wolfpack I'm the leader and that's how it should be, especially with the free-spirit Frenchie who needs a leader of their pack. But I'm also his dad. I'd like to think that I'm a single parent and doing my best to bring him up as a happy, healthy, confident 'kid'. Maybe I'm talking a load of rubbish and Eric doesn't think any of those things at all. Maybe when I call him a doughnut he has his moments when he thinks I'm a doughnut too. But aside from all of that, every day when I'm with Eric I see him look at me and I know he's saying 'thank you'. If he feels loved and at home with me then I'm doing my job properly. I know that Ern and Eric have saved me and just as surely, we saved Eric and brought him home.

Chapter 6

Tender Loving Care

*Keeping your Frenchie
happy and healthy*

THE TRUTH OF it is, the reason for Ern's untimely death was with him before we even met. When I think back over the time we had together, from the moment the vet diagnosed his heart murmur we were living with a ticking timebomb.

Ern could have been one of the lucky ones who just lives with a problem that never shows itself and if it had been that way, we would have enjoyed a good ten, maybe fourteen years together without so much as, well, a murmur. Sadly, we drew the short straw and that long partnership I imagined – where we'd be skipping through the daisies in the park for years (the daisies might be pushing it a bit, but you get the idea) – wasn't to be for us. Generally, Frenchies have good hearts, physically as well as emotionally, and Eric was fit and not overweight – he was just unlucky.

In hindsight, it would have been better to stay indoors that August afternoon and not even attempt a very short walk in the sunshine. I should have played super-safe and not underestimated the warmth in the power of the sun and only taken the boys for a walk in the cool of the early morning or evening. In fact, staying at home altogether would have been the best decision to make. Believe me, all these thoughts ran through my mind in an endless loop after Ern's death: if only I had decided to stay indoors that August afternoon, if only I been more aware of the health danger zones, if only I had realised how severe some of the Frenchie's problems can be ... It could have all been so different.

Ern was a healthy puppy. He was the playful one in the litter and every time I saw him with the breeder he was dancing about trying to play with my shoelaces. He never shied away when I wanted to hold him. I knew these were all good signs and, besides, he looked the perfect little geezer. On that point alone, I wanted him to be mine. I could see us together and I know that sounds more than a bit stupid but that's what it's like when you know you have found the right dog for you.

I can totally understand the popularity of Frenchies but when I meet other Frenchie owners I like to ask them why they love their dogs so much. It turns out it's their baby-like features: the large round eyes and sad expression makes them look so vulnerable and in need of a big, fat hug. We want to protect, nurture and look after them. And it's a very strong emotion – I know because I feel it for Eric and felt it for Ern every single day. After all, they're my boys. Sadly, there are unlucky Frenchie owners who have to nurse their dogs for real.

My experience as a dog lover and then owner has taken me on a long journey and taught me so much I didn't know about Frenchies. I'll admit that I should have known some of these things before I invited Ern into my life but I'm here now and grateful that my little guys forgave me for not always getting it right first time. I now know that all pedigrees and crossbreeds can have sticky health problems that have been passed down from generation to generation until they have become a part of the dogs' genetic make-up. Frenchies, like all dogs with 'flat faces', have inherited a few problems that go with the short nose, big eyes and wrinkles, and they are all things that people who care for and share their lives with these little guys need to be aware of. If you know about them, you can spot the signs of a problem and deal with it right away.

That button, suede nose is part of a Frenchie's loveliness, but it might as well have a sign on it saying: 'Trouble!' When I took Ern for his initial vet consultation I heard the words 'Brachycephalic Obstructive Airway Syndrome' (BOAS) for the first time, and was told all about the condition and how it can affect all flat-nosed breeds. I was listening, I think, but I wish I had asked more questions. The thing is I was so happy to have Ern, at last, and he looked so damn perfect that in my world – otherwise known then as 'cloud nine' – there was no room for worry. Ern was with me and all was right in the universe. It's the old chestnut – if everything is right you don't want to think of anything going wrong. So I didn't. But I had heard enough about 'BOAS' to realise that for as long as I had a Frenchie in my life 'BOAS' would be there too.

It's a combination of problems: narrow nostrils, a long soft palate (an extra-long roof of their mouth) and an underdeveloped windpipe are all in the mix, making life difficult for short-nosed dogs to breathe. In hot weather the breathing problems get a whole lot worse and a Frenchie can get into real trouble catching their breath and, when it really takes hold, there's even a big chance of dying from heatstroke or a heart attack.

Being mindful of respiratory distress is just being sensible, and so is protecting Frenchies from something else they can't cope with: stress. Being in a stressful situation is bad news as it can bring on respiratory distress, forming a vicious circle. They struggle to deal with anxiety and if they get into trouble breathing the stress makes things worse. Believe me, I know how this works and I know the screaming fear that kicks in when your dog goes into respiratory distress. When it happened to Ern I travelled to Hell in a split second. It was a hard lesson for me to learn and one I will never forget.

Sometimes surgery can help ease the problem for Frenchies who have extreme problems just breathing normally. Removing part of the soft palate, will, I'm told, free up the passage of air into the lungs, but putting a dog with breathing problems under anaesthetic is in itself a health risk. Only a vet can advise on whether it's a risk worth taking for the individual. Surgery or no surgery, there is no way you can relax on this front because there is always a need to protect a Frenchie from heat exposure indoors and outdoors, and to make sure they don't get overweight or have too much exercise. If they slip into any of these danger zones they will still often suffer breathing difficulties and stress. There's no way out of this, folks; if you don't follow the rules, the severe consequences will be waiting around the corner for you.

As someone who is wiser after the event of losing Ern, I always have a large jerry can of water in the boot of the car and a pile of towels just in case I need to cool Eric down on the spot if he gets distressed. I'm not taking any chances with him. I'm aware of the dangers and I never want to be in that position again. Eric has regular vet checks to make sure he is a healthy boy. Better to know if there is a bubbling problem so that it can be caught in the early stages.

Regular health checks are pretty much essential with Frenchies because they are prone to these potentially serious problems that can usually only be monitored and managed with veterinary support. That lovely chunky stance the Frenchie pulls off so well is part of their 'look' but it's a heavy body to have resting on such short legs. It's not easy for us owners to detect hip dysplasia so the first clue we get is likely to be seeing our pet limp, appear stiff or look awkward around the rump end as they walk. Same goes if they are having problems with their 'knees' – what your vet will call 'stifles'. Although these conditions are pretty rare they are there in the breed's genetic make-up and if they pop up they won't just go away. It's the same with back problems, which are usually associated with the spinal discs: if one ruptures it can push up into the spinal cord. It even *sounds* painful. And of course it *is* painful and could lead to the sufferer being on anti-inflammatory drugs for life, or even more surgery to stop their back legs becoming totally ineffective – what vets call 'hind-limb paralysis'.

You would think that that's enough to be aware of and contend with but there is another problem that can afflict the Frenchie: Von Willebrand's Disease (VWD for short). This is a blood disorder which affects the blood's ability to clot. The symptoms are a bit more dramatic with this disease and can include nosebleeds, bleeding gums and blood in their poo. If it's not picked up from any of these clues then it's likely it will show itself if the dog has surgery or, in the case of females, bleeding more than usual when they are in season. This is yet another serious condition and not one to shy away from. Any of these symptoms should have you running to the vet for advice. No hanging about and no putting it off.

There are always little jobs we owners have to do to make our dog's life a little more comfortable and the Frenchie owner is kept pretty busy when it comes to maintenance tasks. Those little wrinkles and folds of skin that we love so much are perfectly cute, but they are also little 'shelves' for grime and sweat to collect, fester and develop into something itchy and smelly. Washing between the folds every day with warm water is a good idea but, when you've finished, make sure the skin between the folds is dry. Same goes at bath time. There's no such thing as drip-drying a Frenchie. All those delicate areas need patting dry otherwise they will get sore, itchy and prone to infection.

Take a good long look into those lovely, big round Frenchie eyes and tell me they are not totally freaking adorable! Now look again, without the rose-coloured spectacles, and see how the prominent eyes and shallow sockets can also be a further massive problem area – if you're not careful. Frenchie eyes are exposed and delicate which means that they are prone to infections such as 'cherry eye'. This is when the dog's third eyelid (yes, they have a third eyelid) rolls out to expose the pink fleshy gland underneath, and often needs surgery to fix. This is a painful condition and it can't be allowed to settle in. Bathing the dog's eyes with warm water (use a fresh cotton pad for each eye) every day is so important to help keep this condition at bay.

Watch out for painful eye ulcers too and another disturbing condition called pannus which shows itself as a creeping black film that stretches over the surface of the eyeball. If you see it there, you need to head for the vet right away because pannus is bad news and if it's not caught and treated it will spread and can eventually cause blindness.

And those bat ears? Well, they can kick up a problem if they're not cleaned regularly with warm water on a clean, damp cloth or cotton pad. No need to go poking about with a cotton bud and risk doing more harm than good – just wipe and, most importantly, dry the ear and if you see anything that doesn't look quite right from what you can see down the ear canal, take a trip to the vet to get it checked out. Sometimes the fleshy part of the ear can look a bit dry and cracked but a smear of mineral or baby oil will put that right. The same thing goes for a dry nose – a tiny blob will act as a great moisturiser.

I know this list of ailments sounds like something you'd find on the wall of a vet's surgery with one of those posters with arrows pointing out problems all over a dog's body – all very scary. None of us want to go there, but it's all down to the nature of the breed and it's much better to be aware of the most common health problems because spotting them sooner rather than later can make all the difference to our Frenchies' quality of life.

If you think about it, we do a lot of the DIY health checking without even thinking about it. Cuddling and getting up close to our Frenchies is something we like to do a lot, and they love having the attention so it's not a long stretch to turn that time into an opportunity to carry out a bit of a pet MOT.

Just for one small part of a cuddle session think about what you're doing and run your hands over your dog's body slowly, so you can feel any scars, scabs, lumps, bumps, bald patches, roughness or signs of infection. It's a chance to look and feel for any uninvited guests too. Although Frenchies prefer the great indoors, a walk in the park and a brush through the grass is enough to bring home flea or tick freeloaders. Check nails, teeth, ears and eyes as you go and have a good old bonding session at the same time. Think of it as a spa treatment!

I think Eric is pretty much a typical Frenchie when it comes to liking fuss and attention, so he'll let me check him over and groom him for as long as it takes the cows to come home, have their tea and watch *TOWIE*! Grooming is easy too because Frenchies have a very short coat and no shaggy, lumpy tresses to work through. In fact, it's more of a velvet 'covering' rather than a dog coat so it only takes an occasional brush to keep it looking tip-top and glossy. But if your dog likes being brushed then it's fine to do it more often. If they are having fun and you are happy then it's just another chance to have a bit of 'us' time and relax.

Dogs are masters of relaxation. I think that's part of the magic of sharing your life with them because, even if you try to resist at first, a dog will show you by example the health benefits of slowing down, lying down, kicking your feet in the air and chilling out. Eric is a sleep monster, so any amount of pampering will usually end with him snoring his head off. However, a spa session, Eric-style, doesn't start off relaxed – ever.

If you want to start with him having a bath, well, you can forget it. He'll dodge a bath at any cost – if he can get away with it. The first sound of running water and he's nothing more than a blue blur disappearing to what he thinks is a great hiding place – on my bed. I thought he would have worked out by now that this is the worst 'hiding' place on the planet but then I did say that Eric can be a bit of a doughnut and therefore … I rest my case. But this is all part of what probably looks, to any regular fly on the wall, like a well-rehearsed routine. It goes something like this …

Eric, flat out on his tummy, asleep on my bed. Wakes up when he hears the bath water running, dashes around the flat a bit and then dives back on the bed, taking up a crouched 'hiding' position. I wait until he's settled and thinks I've decided not to bother because the bath water, all two inches of tepidness, has stopped running and then I go and 'find' him. He looks at me as if I'm some kind of axe murderer or public executioner – until I tickle him. Even though he knows what I'm going to do, because I always do the same, he still looks surprised!

The tummy rubs and tickling can go on for a while as he loves it so much and I love to see Eric happy but then, almost as if he knows it's coming to an end, he rolls over onto his side, stands up, legs square apart, ready for me to carry him into the bathroom. He's not a fan of the bathroom, not since we lost Ern. Maybe, like me, he still has images in his head of his big brother lying there on the floor. I can't ever know what Eric is thinking but I know that he goes very quiet when he's in that room, unless you count the usual snuffling and snorting while he's standing in the shallow water – which just about covers his toes. He stands a quick wash and brush-up, without much of a protest every time a lap of water hits his blue-brindle fur, and then I get a look that can only be interpreted as 'I've had enough, mate. If you don't lift me out, I'm jumping out. OK?'

Eric loves the towel-drying much more than the getting wet and Ern was the same. When I had them together they both wanted to be dried off at the same time. It was a wrestle in the water and a wrestle out of the water and, after Ern, Eric put up a good fight on his own! I've always managed to give Eric a health check after a bath. Once I've dried him he's ready to finish off with a good scratch and rub along the rug, and then I can start to check him over for lumps and bumps and he just lies there and lets me get on with it. He stays awake for a while enjoying the fuss and then it's only a matter of time before he starts gradually nodding off – a happy dog. He creases me up. I watch him lying there, his lovely slobbery chops blubbing away with every snore. It happens all the time, but it always makes me smile. Never a dull day, not even a dull moment with Eric around.

Sometimes I think the practical side of owning a dog is like being a caretaker with a lot of maintenance jobs to do: if you keep on top of the niggling things then you won't face too many horrible surprises and expensive breakdowns. It's not so hard to maintain the things that you know will keep your dog healthy and, at the same time, keep away from the things that could do them harm. However, it gets harder to know that you're doing the right thing when your dog is 'different'.

The new array of Frenchie coat colours such as solid black, chocolate, blue, mouse, liver and black with white or tan are bound to attract attention even though they fall outside the breed standard colourings of brindle, fawn and pied. But don't let anyone tell you that they are 'rare' colours as a way of getting you to part with more of your hard-earned cash because there are no such thing as rare colours. Registered breeders will refer to them as 'undesirable' colours and that's because the new colouring makes them an unknown quantity. The fear is that in breeding Frenchies to produce more colour variations there's every chance that some serious health issues have been bred in too.

Ern was a classic red-fawn and Eric is a not-so-classic blue-fawn. Although both colours fall within the breed standard, when you see the boys standing together in photographs, Eric is a much slighter version of the mighty and robust Ernest. Let's say, with his not-so-square head, narrower shoulders and longer back, Eric is a variation on the Frenchie theme. His genetic make-up got shaken up somewhere along the line: maybe within the Hungarian puppy farm that he came from or from the line of his parents – whoever they were. And that's the crux of the health uncertainties for dogs like Eric – the parents' line is unknown and whatever health issues he may develop in his lifetime can't be traced back. Eric will never know who his mum or dad were, and he is unlikely to ever cross paths with his siblings again. If they were beside him in that tobacco lorry leaving Hungary then at least he would have had their company for his rehabilitation at the rescue shelter, but that's all. Eric was a typical product of a puppy farm: a dog with a number not a name, completely anonymous and totally untraceable. But there's one thing Eric has even though he doesn't have a past: he has a great future and his identity can now be traced back to me and our loving home.

I hope Eric feels as happy with me as I am with him because I consider rescuing Eric to be one of my greatest achievements. And although I probably muddled through everything a little bit with Ernest, my 'first born', Eric had the benefit of my acquired knowledge. OK ... let me give you that again, but without the spin: I muddled through less with Eric as a puppy thanks to big Ern being on hand. But there were a few little things I picked up along the way that made life a bit easier for all three of us, especially as we were spending so much time on the road, in other people's company and, sometimes, in the spotlight. And if there's one thing you don't want to share the spotlight with it's … dog drool.

All because of that short nose and flat face, Frenchies drool and they splutter, and when they sneeze you have to get in there quick, tissue in hand, before the landed goo passes the forty-second rule and creates a new pattern on your trouser leg. There's nothing wrong with it, it can't be helped but it's healthier for everyone to keep them clean. I had worn saliva a fair few times before I discovered the benefits of carrying a little 'tool bag' with wipes, tissues, fresh water and a healthy dog treat or two to keep close by – just in case. It's sometimes for my benefit but mostly it's now for Eric so I can dive in if he develops a weepy eye or drippy nose. I register that it could sometimes be down to an allergy, especially if we are outdoors when it starts, but it gives me a chance to clean him up right away. Let's face it, if you don't have something on hand to catch the drool the drool will always find you.

Good mental health is as important for dogs as it

is for people, and if there was an award for the most professional attention-seeker I think Eric would win it every time. Frenchies love attention and that super-sad expression their faces fall naturally into zaps straight to our hearts and we feel we must give them the attention they crave or, should I say, demand. These guys are people pleasers by nature and like to be a lap-warmer more than anything else on earth so it's no surprise that whenever they can't get that attention they suffer terrible separation anxiety. To be happy and healthy, Frenchies need us to be around them.

When Ern first came to me we were in each other's shadow virtually 24/7. When I couldn't take him to the office with me, or later, on location shoots with *TOWIE*, he had my lovely Nan for company and that worked fine. What began to stress him out was the lack of routine in his life: he had shared a routine of a kind with me but then even that was turned on its head with the TV commitments. Once the extreme anxiety kicked off it was there in Ern's behaviour. He wasn't pacing like a polar bear in a zoo, but he was biting and licking his paws and he was jittery. I hated seeing how it was starting to affect his health. That old soul of a dog was missing something and the change in routine was making him anxious. It was thanks to Eric, the fun guy's arrival, that Ern's stress disappeared. As a bit of a loner at heart, I'm always amazed by the power of companionship and dogs seem to have it sorted perfectly.

If it helps to know, I've read that Frenchies are, overall, the healthiest of the bulldog breeds. Now, although that's no guarantee of a 100 per cent trouble-free life, there's no need to get paranoid about the potential of a bit of bother. Knowledge is power and being aware of the signs of the most common conditions to affect Frenchies is half the battle won. Then you can let your vet do the rest.

My Frenchies are my own little family, and now that it's just me and Eric I'm probably a lot more observant than I used to be when it comes to his health. And yes, I would do anything to make sure that he doesn't go through what Ern suffered but I'm up against a challenge with Eric's undocumented past. I try not to be nervous or think too much about it, and I try really hard sometimes not to obsess. Although, on a bad day that's a lot easier said than done. But worrying about your dog is all part and parcel of being a responsible owner, as any parent of a child will tell you too. And in the end it's a small price to pay for the unwavering devotion you get in return.

Chapter 7

Are You Talking to Me?

Training tips

YOU KNOW I love Ern and Eric with all my heart, but just recently my mum reminded me that I was only four years old when I lost my heart for the first time. I wracked my brain trying to work through the names of girls in my class at school and then narrowed it down to the ones I would have first met at nursery or playschool. The more names mum rejected the more my mind blanked out. That's it ... I give up. 'What was her name, Mum?' The answer wasn't what I expected. Apparently, the love of my life's name was sometimes Beethoven, other days Tramp or Pongo, but that could change to any one of the dozens of dogs' names dreamt up by the Disney film studios. And it turns out that my *very* first love was on wheels and made of wood and was also the best-behaved dog anyone could ever have.

I loved all the Disney films about animals: *The Fox and the Hound* was my favourite followed by *The Incredible Journey*, *Aristocats*, *101 Dalmatians* and the series based on a dynasty of St Bernard dogs called *Beethoven*. You name one and I will have watched it at least a million times over. I'd watch one now if it popped up on TV! So, there I was in a world of my own, watching films about talking animals and every time changing the name of my wooden toy to match the name of the hero on screen. My little dog on wheels was so patient and never suffered a name identity crisis or complained about me holding him so close that I had dents in my skin.

I slept with him, ran with him, talked to him and generally never let go of him. His floppy brown leather ears, springy tail with a green ball on the end and cream, beagle-like body with one painted black spot were all scarred by my affections. According to my mum, I trundled the dog along on the short length of stripy rope from dawn to dusk until his wheels became worn down. I even used to bite chunks out of his body. I'm told I refused to give him up at nap time and bath time – I can't imagine a wooden toy being that comfy to curl up with, but this one obviously was, to me. He was my closest friend.

I loved that dog to pieces, literally, and when I recall Ern's steadfast loyalty and see Eric acting a bit daft, I think of where it all began with my first dog – my pal on wheels. That dog loved all the walks but didn't need feeding, grooming, vaccinating, training or a bed of his own. I didn't need to cater for his welfare needs or consider his moods and personality traits and he was just everything I needed him to be – totally devoted to me. My mum still has him stored away safe and sound forever, but thinking about him after all these years I wonder how many Frenchie fanciers think taking on a real dog is just as hassle-free. And of course my wooden pal was incredibly well behaved and sensible – not like all real dogs, unfortunately.

When I say that Eric is the joker in the Wolfpack I say it with total respect. If I ever crack a joke at his expense, then be sure that I'm laughing with him and never at him. Ernest was the same. He would smile at Eric, in his own protective big brother kind of way; even when Eric did something spectacularly daft, Ern still looked on proudly. I'll admit he had THAT look sometimes, though – the one where his face slumped and he looked like he was sighing: 'Eric, you're such a doughnut sometimes, but I still love you ...'

It's not that Eric behaves badly; it's more that he's a natural entertainer, which can sometimes turn him into his own version of Captain Chaos. It happens when we're out and about because Eric doesn't do boundaries and he stomps all over the idea of personal space. So other dogs can be minding their own business sniffing what they want to sniff and licking what they want to lick and suddenly there's Eric right in their grill begging to join in! He's always desperate to make friends and he can't see how it could all end in tears, getting him into a scrap. I hate seeing this happen to Eric because he is a real top geezer who just wants to get on with everyone and can't compute why everyone makes it so difficult. I've watched this so often now and I reckon there's nothing wrong with what he's trying to do. It's just that he's going about it all the wrong way – and he can't take the heaviest of hints.

Let me give you an example ... my mum's cat hates Eric. However, Eric doesn't seem to have got the message. Every time we go around to mum's he spends the whole time trying to convince Muppet, the cat, that she must like him *really*. He sits in her shadow, less than two feet away from her, and she hisses at him! He gets in her face – and she hisses at him! He sidles up to her when he thinks she's not looking, – and she hisses at him! And what does Eric do? He just sits there and takes it all. He's obsessed with that bad-tempered black-and-white cat and can't understand why she doesn't give a damn about him!

This little scenario is played out every time they meet, and every time Eric is determined to make Muppet see his good side while she is determined to remind him that she loathes him. It's as if time and repeated rejection has taught him absolutely nothing. I've got to admit that a small part of me admires Eric's resilience and I'm a little bit envious of the huge swell of hope that he has in his heart. But, at the same time, I can't help wondering if this cycle of optimism and determination followed by rejection is down to him being emotionally thick-skinned or just plain thick?

Maybe if Eric could find a girlfriend he wouldn't be so desperate to make friends with Muppet ... but I'm not so sure. I think he'd still give it a try. I don't think it's down to lack of self-esteem: instead I have a feeling that he's so full of love to give that he can't help over-sharing. That's it – Eric is an 'over-sharer', forcing his beautiful slobbering friendship on other dogs and people. Let's face it, he's a Frenchie, so what else should I expect? He has a lovely big heart and while Ernest was very choosy about his friendships, and chose to be close only to me and my Nan, Eric, in comparison, is the very definition of over-pally. He wants to have a special bond – with everyone! Having a huge heart is a great thing but wanting to share the love 24/7 is not so easy, especially as Eric just keeps getting it wrong.

As you know by now, our adventures in the park can be a bit eventful and Eric never seems to learn from his mistakes. I've told him that running up to other dogs and randomly sniffing their bums is not the best way to make friends, but he always thinks he knows better. The park is the best place to see the best and worst in dog behaviour, and dogs off the lead are always a scary unknown quantity – especially when their owner is nowhere to be seen.

The day Eric came off worse in one of his too-close-for-comfort encounters was a day I won't forget. If it hadn't been for Ernest I think the episode would have had a very unhappy ending and it was all down to an invisible and, yes, I'm going to say it, irresponsible dog owner.

From the day that Eric was old enough to go on walks with us I could see that Ern was getting the measure of our new recruit. I'm sure he could tell that Eric was all bustle, bounce and very little brain, especially in social situations, so he took it upon himself to become his little brother's shadow. There was nothing funnier than watching this play out when we were in the park and every time I watched them together I became more and more convinced that as long as Ern was around, everything would be OK.

If the coast was clear I'd let the pair of them wander off the lead for a while and, every now and then, call them back to me just to make sure they hadn't forgotten the sound of my voice and the joys of recall, which meant they would get some fuss and praise in return. My boys never misplaced my trust and always kept close to me while rooting about and doing all the things dogs do. I cleaned up after them and kept a general eye on things until it was time to round them up and make our way home.

I felt myself smiling as I watched the two of them snuffling about and doing their usual sniffs and sneezes and puddle-dodging. That day I was in my own proud dad mode when suddenly, out of nowhere, another dog – a huge German shepherd, no less – dashed up looking for some action. Eric was on it like a car bonnet, giving the interloper the full-on Eric 'let's play' treatment. He was weaving and panting, hopping up and down on his front paws and trying to attract the big dog's attention. I could tell Eric was thinking, 'Surely the new guy wants to play? What have I got to do to make him join in?'

What happened next happened very quickly and I think we all knew that from the moment the other dog appeared it could go a sniff too far – and it did. The German shepherd, clearly irritated by Eric's antics, started eyeing him like he was dinner and I knew that we were only one false move away from the bigger dog going in for an attack.

Ernest saw every move and being a true pro judged his moment to step in with pure perfection. It was like the famous stand-off scene in the old black-and-white Gary Cooper Western, *High Noon,* and for more than a few seconds I held my breath. I couldn't move my feet, but my eyes were busy scanning the area for the owner of the German shepherd, who was, of course, nowhere in sight. The only thing Eric had on his side was that the Wolfpack outnumbered the opposition three to one.

Ernest knew what to do. He squared up to the bigger guy with his signature 'look', which plainly said: 'Don't mess with the Wolfpack.' He took a series of half-steps forward in what I think must be the best version of Frenchie intimidation I'm sure I will ever see. It was enough to get the dog to swap his attention from Eric and onto Ern. In the split second that the two dogs had eye contact I thought we were in trouble. But I should have known better and given Ern due credit – he stood his ground until the other dog turned tail and ran away. The stand-off was over, and no one was hurt. Thanks to good old Ern.

Eric's behaviour worries me sometimes. His over-friendliness is kind of cute but every now and then I want to ask him: 'Don't I love you enough, mate? Surely you don't need to burst your way into other people's affections the way you do?' I don't want to sound super-sensitive but there are times when I can get a bit upset about this, but I always come to the same conclusion … it's in his nature. Just as it was in Ern's nature to square up to any dog who fancied their chances against the Wolfpack. I have no doubt that he would have done whatever was needed to protect us, but for all Ern's evil looks and thrusting chest movements it was only ever for show. He was never the aggressor. Ern was just instinctively standing up for his family and I was always there as the leader and protector to make sure nothing happened, and no one was hurt.

Ern's over-protective behaviour has been part of his personality since he was a puppy – in fact when he was just twelve months old he showed what kind of mighty courage he was made of in the face of a perceived threat. He was staying with my nan at the time which, for me, made what happened all the worse because it upset her and that's the last thing I would ever want to do. My granddad Patrick loved to take Ern for walks, but he always felt happier keeping him on his lead and that was fine by me. I totally understood where he was coming from although I knew, without a shadow of a doubt, that if he let him off the lead, Ern would never have run away or got into any trouble. No matter what Ern was doing – relaxing at home or out on a walk – he had one priority and that was to stay close to and protect the person alongside him. But I understood why Granddad Pat would want to keep him close; I didn't want anyone to worry about Ern running away or anything like that. I wanted Nan and Patrick to enjoy having him around and just relax in his company because I knew they could. But that day they saw a different side of 'Ern the adorable' when a flash of 'Ern the don't mess with me!' made an appearance!

According to Granddad Pat, they were walking along perfectly happily. Ern jogged jauntily ahead, as he always did, setting his own little pace for his walker to follow. Suddenly a German shepherd (yes, another one), who was off the lead, appeared in front of them. Whatever happened next ended with Ernest losing a chunk out of one ear. Sounds like the other dog got too close too quickly and Ern wasn't having any of it. His priority was to protect my granddad from the attacker – not that all nineteen stone and six foot four of Pat needed protecting but it wouldn't have looked like that to Ern, who let out a victory snort and snuffle as the loose dog ran away. I know my nan was upset that it happened, but Ern was doing his duty and the person he was with was unhurt. Proof, if proof was ever needed, that you don't mess with Ray Winstone!

Frenchies are big softies but never mistake their big-heartedness for cowardice. These guys don't look for trouble, but they won't shy away if it's shoved in their faces. They will defend and protect their territory and their loved ones, just as Ern did in the park, so you know there's enough of the bulldog instinct left in their behaviour traits to back up that solid macho exterior. Having said all of that, what Frenchies really want to do is not get stroppy but get comfy, whether on someone's lap or stretched out on their owner's bed or sofa. They seek peace and not war, so why do they get into trouble with other dogs?

If you go to certain clubs and pubs at a certain time on a Saturday night, then you can almost expect a bit of agg. You can be minding your own business, hanging out with friends and enjoying yourself without a care in the world and then you walk into one particular bar and suddenly the atmosphere changes. There are lots of glances in different directions and then you realise that all the focus has fallen on you – you just don't know why. All you know is that your face doesn't fit and there's nothing you can do about it. What do you do when the others look so fierce? Do you run, or do you stay and stare it out? Frenchies face this kind of dilemma all the time just because of their looks. The trouble, as I mentioned earlier, is that other dogs can't read them.

Frenchies are tailless, flat faced and have big, bulging eyes. All lovely features to their owners, perfection as far as my Ern and Eric are concerned, but for other dogs these looks often appear to be just plain confusing. Just as we 'read' other people's body language for clues to their temperament – and to judge if they look friendly or aggressive – dogs size up others when they approach. They have just a short time to gather in all the signs, anticipate what could happen next and prepare an appropriate response. It all happens in a flash, but a Frenchie's mix of features seems to stop that fast-tracking process dead. When a dog can't compute the other dog's mood, then it's usually time to make a choice – fight or take flight?

I really wish that other breeds of dog could learn just to walk away if they meet a Frenchie, because these big personalities in a small dog's body won't hurt a fly. They are generally well behaved, love people and don't pick fights with other dogs but they will defend and protect their loved ones till their last breath. It's a quality in their behaviour that I admire and respect and remember fondly about Ernest. He had a presence that shouted out loud: 'I'm here. You don't have to like me but if you try to mug off my family I'll be down on you like a load of bricks, my son!'

Behaviour is closely linked with intelligence – well, that's what some of the people 'in the know' would say – but I think Frenchies are brainier than they are given credit for. According to Stanley Coren's *The Intelligence of Dogs*, Frenchies are ranked in fifty-eighth place for overall breed intelligence but there have been many times when I would have given the number one spot to Ernest, and even Eric, on one of his less daft days, would make the top ten. I swear that my dogs understand every word I say. And they are clever enough to adopt a convincing case of selective hearing if they don't like the sound of something I ask them to do! Eric can become particularly hard of hearing when I tell him to get off the bed. And Ern could blot out the sound of me rattling the lead if he fancied sleeping in instead of a morning walk.

But they are not alone in their intelligence: I read that a Frenchie called Princess Jacqueline, who died in 1934, had a recorded understanding of twenty words. That's impressive for a breed that some people call the clown of the dog world!

I have a feeling that Frenchies know exactly what's going on and they have us totally sussed. These bulky independent individuals want us to believe that they are a tiny bit stupid because it suits them. And that's where basic training is a must in all dog breeds, but especially for Frenchies as it's so important to narrow the gap between well behaved and free spirited. Dog-training classes recommended by your vet are a good place to work together to develop your dog's skills and that's true of older dogs as well as puppies. Contrary to popular belief, you *can* teach an older dog new tricks and taking the road together is the best way to develop that all-important trust. Day by day, bit by bit, the training will pay off and a well-behaved dog will emerge.

How to get started?

First find the tasty incentive that your dog will always enjoy as a reward for good behaviour. Most dogs will hang on your every word for a tiny morsel of cooked chicken, ham or sausage. Something strong-smelling (not spicy) and no bigger than half the size of your little fingernail. It will look small to you, but it's only meant to be a tiny reward for doing as they are asked, not a chance to hand out extra portions. In this case small is best. And to get the best out of your mini-training sessions, separate them from proper meal times and natural sleep times so you are working with a wide-awake pupil who wants to earn that treat from you.

Some dogs prefer to work for extra fuss rather than food and if your dog is prone to being overweight then it's definitely better to try this approach. If a back scratch is the way to your dog's heart, then you have the perfect reward at your fingertips. The same for dogs who have a favourite toy. But if that's the way for you to go, best set that particular plaything aside for training only, so it doesn't get mixed in with the everyday collection and lose its special status. It must be a prize worth winning. All you have to remember with the toy is to throw or present it at the exact moment you 'mark' your dog's correct behaviour. That way the two are always associated with each other. And your 'marker'? Well, that can be a clicker (you could ask your vet or local dog trainer about using a clicker) or any command, chosen by you, to 'mark' your dog's success. You could make this an enthusiastic 'Yes!' or 'Good pup!' said with lots of oomph as you offer the tasty reward, toy or praise.

Don't shout! All the commands must be spoken softly so there's no confusion and the little bubble of focus and attention isn't broken and, more importantly, the trust isn't lost. Shouting is a bad thing to do, so if your pup doesn't get what you're saying, stop the session and try again later when you can keep your cool. Think about it, would you want to toe the line if someone shouted at you and told you what to do? I doubt it. I know it would have the reverse effect on me so why should we expect a dog to be any different? This is positive reward-based training. It's the only way to go and it's never an excuse to show who's boss. Get this training right and your dog will learn the basics for life through nurtured trust and respect. Believe me, it's the only way to build the lasting bond you want with your dog.

Keep the sessions short and sweet. Frequent and fun is the best way to approach the training, especially with a puppy. If you push and push for longer sessions your dog will lose interest, get bored and look for something else to do such as chew something unsuitable or just fall asleep. It won't matter how much yummy grub you have in your pocket to reward your dog with if they are tired. Best to call time and try again later or the next day. Be patient. No loving, trusting partnership can grow under pressure. And if you're not careful, you will find you are talking to yourself with only a bagful of cooked sausage bits for company.

Lesson one: 'Sit!' Gather all the patience you can muster and get set to repeat every session several times. Stock up on your chosen tasty treat and prepare to be amazed! Teaching your pup to 'sit' is kind of dog-speak for 'please'. It's the foundation stone for every command that follows. They must learn this one before they can do anything more enjoyable so get this right and you're onto a winner.

As this is the first and most important of lessons I'll share this one with you. It worked really well for me and my boys (with the help of a bag of crispy bacon bits), so here goes ...

1. Hold the chosen treat in your hand.
2. Hold your treat-filled hand by your dog's nose so they can take a good whiff and get interested.

3. As they sniff, move your hand upwards and see how, like magic or magnetism, the dog's head follows. Then move your hand slowly back from your dog's nose and towards the back of their head – so their head lifts and, at the same time, their bottom goes to the floor.

4. As their bottom touches the ground, say 'Sit!' Then say your 'marker', which for me was 'Yes! Good boy!' and hand over the treat or deliver the praise, whatever works best for your dog.

5. Then say 'OK!' which releases them from the situation.

6. Repeat. You're looking for around five 'sits' from your dog to show that they've got the gist of it.

7. Next, you're looking to get the 'sit' position with a little less performance. So go through the same motions but this time say 'Sit!' just *before* you move your hand, but all in the same motion.

8. As your dog sits, say 'Yes!' and deliver the treat.

9. Repeat this a few more times ... and then take a break.

I remember feeling a bit like a magician performing a trick when I did this for the first time with Ern and I was so impressed with the speed of his reactions as he got to grips with what he was learning. I appreciate that I was, in Ern's terms, just playing a game and handing out bacon bits, but for me as a newbie dad and dog owner it was bloody amazing! It really feels like you are bonding with your dog. I remember saying to Ern, once we had cracked the 'sit' stage, that I couldn't be prouder of him. Anyone who thinks Frenchies are in any way stupid needs their own head looking at, in my opinion. These dogs are just the best, but then I am biased.

Even free-thinker Eric was a good lad when it came to training him to 'sit' on command. The offer of bacon bits probably had a lot to do with it but that's how it goes, and it's often a case of doing whatever it takes to make it work for both of you. No one wants an ill-mannered dog, and that's what you have a good chance of rearing if you don't put in the time to establish the basics of 'sit' and recall.

So, carrying on ...

Lesson two: 'Heel!' In dog-speak this means 'come to my side', which is what you need your dog to do when you call them to you. They should walk at your side or, as the professionals call it, 'walk to heel'. This is to make sure that wherever you are you are in control of your dog. Which in turn means they are less likely to get into trouble and will always do as you ask. If the two of you can get this second basic skill under your belt, then you have a partnership in the making.

Here's how Ern and Eric learnt to walk to heel ...

1. Hold your tasty treat or toy at the heel position – which depends on your dog's height – so level with your ankle/knee/thigh and make sure your dog can see you have it there. Call them to this hand and as they reach you give them the treat. You have now established the hand signal for the command.

2. Try this same movement in different places (for example at home, in the park), and after five or six successes introduce the word 'heel' as you deliver their reward.

3. Then start to say 'heel' as they come towards you, so the word is associated with 'arriving' in position.

4. Walk at heel and stay in position.

5. When your dog arrives in the heel position take a couple of steps forward and reward them as you're walking. Build this up to longer distances giving the rewards while they stay in the heel position.

6. Next push the boundaries by asking them to come to heel as they go past a place where they would normally be distracted or try to pull away from you. Then reward them by allowing them to go and investigate – and then call them back to heel.

7. Remember, 'heel' is the word you say when you want your dog to come to your side and stay. It doesn't matter where they are when you call them, they should come to you and stay at your side no matter if you are standing still or walking with them. The idea is to teach your dog to go longer distances at heel, ignoring the usual distractions, all for a treat. Eventually, you will be able to do this with the treat hidden and just on your word of command.

I realise that seeing this written down looks a bit scary and straight out of the rigid rule book but, to be honest, it's just common sense with some expert technique thrown in. Dogs need to have boundaries and to know what is acceptable and they look to their owner to set the rules. I did all of this for my benefit as well as the boys because I knew that it was the right thing to do, but we kind of developed our own version of what looks like a prescription approach. The result was two well-mannered dogs in a trusting relationship, which is what I believe it is all about. The thing is we, as responsible dog owners, have to start somewhere, and this basic training is a great way to get to know your dog as well as yourself.

The other thing to remember is that training a dog involves the whole family. One adult can take the job on at first because that's best for the dog. It helps with continuity and all-important consistency, and avoids mixed messages. But after that everyone else in the family must follow the rules that have been set from the start. Confusing your dog will make it all a waste of time for everyone and destroy any trust you will have built up along the way.

Teamwork is at the heart of everything you invest in your dog's behaviour training. It's about everyone working to the same plan to deliver the same message and offer the same reward. Consistency and clarity will give your pup or more mature dog confidence and reassurance, so they are able to hit the outside world equipped with socially acceptable behaviour. Everyone loves a dog with good manners. And they're not so keen on a dog without them.

I can see now that to stand any chance of success, owners need to get their own act together for their dog's sake. Dogs are very sensitive to our feelings so if you are uptight or unsure when you are training together that wobbliness will transmit down the lead to the dog. Horses are the same and if they detect that the person holding the reins isn't quite up to the job then the fun and games will start! They know when they have an idiot up top and, given the opportunity, they can be pretty unforgiving. Underestimating other animals' intelligence is a huge human failing. I know it often feels like I'm the leader in our Wolfpack but I'm not arrogant enough to think I'm the only one that matters in the relationship. Training with Ern and Eric was to benefit all three of us and ultimately everyone we would ever meet along the way.

And the learning never really stops. I know I was a latecomer to the whole world of responsible dog ownership so please forgive me if I sound like some pop-up 'dog evangelist' or one of those annoying ex-smokers spouting discovered wisdom, but I now know that the standard of a dog's behaviour is in the hands of their owner. If my experience is anything to go by you can learn to do a good job – if you want to.

Reading up, asking questions and not giving up when things appear challenging help boost confidence and we all know that self-confidence is a winner in every walk of life – even dog ownership. Finding out what is expected of you as a responsible dog owner is important and knowledge encourages confidence, as well as helping you set boundaries at home and get to grips with teaching basic commands. That done, the pecking order gets established – so you are always seen as the one in charge and not the dogs – and the rest you work out together. It's what happened with me, Ern and Eric. If there's one big lesson that I have learnt so far, it's that we owe it to our dogs to be the best people we can be for them – in every way.

It started with me wanting Ern to be happy, healthy and comfortable in his new life and home and we kind of got that covered quite quickly, including him finding his comfy spot – on my bed. And because I was still in my selfish phase I not only wanted an instantly well-behaved dog (clearly, I was still thinking of my impeccably behaved wooden dog on wheels) but I also wanted him to look the part too.

I don't mind admitting that I like to look smart and I have probably been guilty of putting flashness before comfort on more than one occasion – even long before my days on *TOWIE* – so when I prepared for Ern's arrival I bought all the usual gear including some fashionable, but only borderline practical, collars and leads. My boy dog was going to have boy gear and that's as far as my head took me. But for all their Frenchie cuteness and lazy, lapdog reputation, these dogs are muscular little guys and I soon realised that safety and control on the lead was more important than I first thought.

It turns out that a lead is not just a lead when it's a piece of kit and body support. When a friend introduced me to the wonders of the dog harness it didn't take me long to discover that nothing could be better for supporting the solid frame of a Frenchie on the move. That big head, broad chest and long back resting on those short legs makes quite a chunk of dog to control and keep hold of, and I could see that Ern was instantly happier in a harness. When my mate recommended a 'padded' version it meant Ern's underarms were protected too. That was really important because we can forget those little hidden areas where a Frenchie's coat is at its thinnest. They are short of hair all over but it's super-short over their tummy and chest. In their macho harnesses my boys looked top geezers and I felt I had control not only of the fashion situation but the need for comfort too. I was learning – there was a responsible dog owner inside me after all – and it felt good.

I don't see how any of us can ever be 100 per cent sure that we are getting it right all the time but if we do our best we've done all we can. Sharing a home with Ern and Eric was like sharing with my mates. The only difference being, with the dogs, I didn't have to suffer all the boy banter about my hair and my height! The flat is our home, our space, our castle and when there were three of us we were all well-behaved there and respectful to each other's needs ... but goodness help anyone who tried to invade our territory! Good old boy Ern was the self-appointed guard dog. He would have barked if he had ever been really worried by genuine intruders, but he always made his presence felt in a snorting, snuffling, square-dog kind of way every time someone came to the door. I never stopped him or even discouraged him because he was defending his territory and he always came to heel when I asked him to. He was a very well-behaved guard dog who was probably rather disappointed in Eric who still sleeps through any domestic disturbance to this day. I'm sure he would give a burglar a very savage lick on the hand – before going back to bed!

I respect my boys as dogs with needs all of their own and I respect and love them as individual personalities. I think it's what you have to do when you are responsible for someone else as well as yourself. I'm not so sure everyone who invites a dog to share their life and space realises that they are making one of the most serious decisions of their life. I didn't. Back in the day, as far as I was concerned, I was just adding a dog into the mix but other than that everything would remain the same. No ripples in my pond. What I didn't appreciate, until Ern was peeing on the rug, chewing chair legs and sprawling on my bed, was that he had needs all of his own. And if we were going to live in perfect harmony, it was my responsibility to fulfil every single one of them – or not be a dog owner.

My behaviour and his behaviour were now entwined, and we had a home life, social life and work life together, so I had to think ahead for Ern as well as myself to make sure everything ran smoothly – especially when we were in company. For a little while, things ran anything but smoothly because Ern, all-round fabulous guy that he was, wasn't born well behaved. We had to work on that together and the result was a partnership, a man/dog team, the making of the Wolfpack, which was built entirely on trust.

It was a beautiful thing we made and, I think, my greatest achievement. The arrival of Eric was the cherry on the top and I was happy – with a capital 'H'.

I have never regretted inviting Ern and Eric into my life. Well, that's not entirely true: maybe in the first twenty-four hours after Ern arrived, when everything descended into chaos, I wondered what on earth I had done! But huge waves of love and protection soon washed all the doubt away and we were ready to do some serious male bonding. In a way I was lucky that I didn't have to start from scratch with Ern. He had already started on his socialisation journey when he came to me; he wasn't freaked out by travelling in a car or the sound of the vacuum cleaner, the TV or the kettle boiling so we had some foundations to build on. He was mine to mould. Only time would tell if he had inherited some issues with his temperament, but all looked good from the start: he was happy, laid back, willing to learn and wanted to be with me wherever I went – even to the bathroom! I didn't mind; he was my boy.

But then came Eric – a rescue dog and an unknown quantity in every way. There was only one way we were going to find out if he had inherited any issues and that was by living with him, giving him all the love, care and basic training we could and seeing what happened along the way. The local dog shelter's socialisation team didn't report anything to worry about, only a few endearing little habits like sucking on your clothing and burrowing his head into your body to get closer to you. But then he would, wouldn't he? After being taken so early from his mum he was probably still looking for her every time he was handled. It's all second-guessing because rescue dogs like Eric are little mysteries on four legs and part of the joy of having them around is peeling away the layers to reveal glimpses of their true story. They are packed with surprises. One thing that still surprises me about Eric is that he particularly likes snuggling into anyone who has the smell of tobacco on their clothes. Weirdly, he doesn't appear to hate the smell after his long, illegal journey from Hungary to the UK in a tobacco lorry. Perhaps there's more to that little episode than I'll ever know but I'll carry on gathering the clues if it can help him in his new life with me. If only dogs could talk. We all say it, don't we? Even if there was one day a year when they could answer our questions, tell us how they are feeling and what they would like or what we are doing wrong, it would be mint! Or at least we think it would be because it would help us do a better job of unravelling the torment of our rescue dogs and reassure us that we are doing all the right things to make our dogs happy, healthy and confident in our world.

We know that what we put into a dog is what we are likely to get out, and that's because how they behave is not all down to the traits they were born with. Their temperament and behaviour are also down to us as responsible dog owners and how we nurture and shape them as individuals through training, love and respect.

And there's no excuse because if you're looking for any kind of guidance and self-help on the internet you will never be short of sources. Trouble is … who is right and who will send you barking up the wrong tree? It's the same with healthy diet and lifestyle advice – you must talk to your vet. There's no compromise on this; it's like finding a good school for your child. The pressure should be on to get it right first time because the consequences of messing up can be dire.

When it comes to behaviour training for a dog it must always be based on kindness, positivity and reward. There is no place for cruelty or any form of punishment. All of that, wherever it exists, is outdated, totally negative and plain wrong. A well-behaved dog is not the product of human domination or control. Good owners, who follow approved and respected guidance on reward-based, positive reinforcement training will find that their dog's respect for them develops naturally. You're in this together and that's where the trust comes in. Once you share trust with your dog, you have it all and you'll never need to look back.

I remember the first time I took Ern on the train to work. Part of me felt like an excited schoolboy taking my most prized possession into class for a 'Show and Tell' session! I wanted to show him off to my work colleagues. He was so handsome, smart and well behaved. The other part of me was hoping that I wouldn't, at some point along the journey, wonder what the hell had made me think this was such a great idea.

When Ern took his first steps onto the train that morning he did it with all the confidence of a well-honed heavyweight boxer entering the ring at Madison Square Garden. He was confidence on a stick. He was the dog's bollocks – you know what I mean? I could feel myself almost strut with pride as if his confidence had rubbed off on me.

The women on the train adored him, even the blokes adored him! Ern was a star. He took that journey with me many times after that day and he was always the perfect passenger: he never made a mess (he slobbered on a few people, but they were happy to be slobbered on, so that was OK), never hogged a seat, never left us reeling from the smell of sweaty armpits and never left the pages of the *Metro* strewn all over the floor of the carriage.

Walking from Tower Hill station to the offices I would often have to stop to speak to fellow dog lovers and walkers and passers-by who just couldn't resist breaking their power-walk to work to stroke Ernest. Some would call it animal magnetism; I think it was just the magic of Ern. He made people smile.

Every day he went into the office with me was a better day for everyone. He wowed my office colleagues from the moment he entered the building. He walked beside me, sat with me and was my work buddy. We did everything on trust and saw the training pay off massively. Like a proud dad I felt I had made it when one of the team said to me: 'You must be very proud of Ernest; he's a credit to you, Pete. A real credit.'

Honest to God, that brought a tear to my eye.

Excuse a touch of the bromantic here but when I reached this stage with Ern and then Eric I could feel the power of trust in the Wolfpack. They were right beside me and being there for them made me feel that we were set for a true happy ever after.

Do you know, there's one quality in dogs that I admire more than any other – they live for the moment. They respond instinctively to things that make them happy, angry or sad because everything, as far as they are concerned, is in the 'now'. Rescue dogs, even the ones that have been ill treated and had their trust completely trashed by people, can still respond to kindness. The touch of a kind hand and the sound of a soft, kind voice will find the love in them, even if they have never felt it before.

Look at Eric. Born on a puppy farm, he lived his early life in darkness and squalor. Denied food, water and care then ripped away from his mum before he could properly fend for himself. Most likely drugged and then transported thousands of miles from where he was born in Hungary to be sold by a third-party seller here in the UK at any price: an object for sale. In the kind hands of the rescue centre staff Eric found love and gave love. Pure and honest. I sometimes wish we could be that candid and keep things so simple but human beings always introduce complications. Someone would always want more, and greed would mess it all up. And there would probably be a fight!

This, in my view, is where dogs are often let down by people. Dogs are dogs and need their owners to work with them to develop good manners and socially acceptable behaviour. In my mind, there's never a badly behaved dog, only an owner who couldn't be bothered to put the time in. People really need to stop blaming dogs for their own mistakes. It really winds me up. When I see someone losing their nut because their dog has embarrassed them, I want to shout over: 'Mate, stop blaming your dog – it's your fault. Knobhead!'

I don't trust people with my dogs. No, that's not entirely true. I trust *some* people with my dogs. But I trust my dogs in everyone's company and I'm so proud of them and how we have grown as a little family. I've often said that I prefer Ern and Eric's company to most people and anyone who knows me will say that's true. Don't get me wrong, the party boy is always there on the surface but deep down, given the choice between a night on the town and a couch potato slob-in with Eric, I'd choose the time with Eric. Maybe it's because I feel I have a better connection with dogs than I do with people. Maybe it's because I know that I can be myself with Eric and he'll think that's absolutely enough for him.

Is it a case of 'love me, love my dogs'? Yes, it always will be. Ern and Eric are part of my life and even though Ern is not here, in person, he is still part of who I am now and so, in every way, the Wolfpack lives on.

After Ern's passing I have become more aware of how responsible owners are for their dog's health and welfare, and that includes how they behave with other dogs and interact with people. They rely on us to get it right. If we screw them up, then we only have ourselves to blame.

Chapter 8

Ern's Legacy

*How the Wolfpack changed
my life*

WHENEVER SOMEONE ASKS me why I love Frenchies, I can feel my brain click into a part of me that now belongs – and will forever belong – to Ern and Eric. It's as if having their companionship has developed an extension of me as a person, and I will always be grateful to them for coming into my life and becoming the better part of me.

Whenever we were out as the Wolfpack, people would stop me in the street and ask why I like Frenchies so much. They assumed that because I've chosen two dogs of the same breed that I not only love my Frenchies, but that I know a lot about them too. Well, I certainly know more now than three years ago, and it was probably obvious that I was proud of myself striding along, with Ern and Eric jogging next to me on the end of a lead. If asked, I had no trouble gushing about my dogs – my funny, smart, loyal best friends. A couple of top geezers …, that's my boys. I must have sounded like a first-time dad of twins or something. I could hear myself say these words and would give myself the OK for being my own dogs' number one fan. And why not? I was happy then. Walking on air with Ern and Eric at my side.

In life after Ern, when I'm asked the same question, I feel myself pause a little before I answer. With the Wolfpack a member down do I feel differently now? No, I don't, because Eric is my best mate; he is loyal, funny, inspirational and has a heart of gold. I still feel all those same feelings; it's just that they shine on half-power without Ern. He had a special strength to share with me which came from knowing who I was: he was there to give me an injection of confidence if I needed it, and if I needed to talk something through he was always ready to listen. I'm a great believer that talking to your dog doesn't look as odd as talking to yourself. I hope that's right because I talked to Ern a lot and I know that dog understood every word I said.

Frenchies are the best! I know what you are going to say – everyone says their dog is the best, and so they should, whatever the breed. Since becoming a dog owner, I have met some fantastic people who love their pets so much they would die for them. And I'm not joking. I've met dog owners who would go without things themselves to make sure their dog had the right food and the best of care. It's very humbling to meet people like that who sacrifice without thinking. And when it comes to Frenchie folk, well, they are pure gold. I have been made so welcome into the fold. Every time I go to one of the breed events I have such a lot of fun and that's one of the wonderful things about people who love dogs: they are all such lovely people. Without my Frenchies I would never have met them and that would have been a sad loss.

Frenchie people are like their dogs: bright, happy, alert, playful, affectionate and fun-loving. When they get together in their fan clubs or at fundraising events they generate an energy. It's like they attack life with the attitude that every day could be their last and the days are too short to be miserable. It's great to be a part of because everyone is smiling – even the dogs! But then having a Frenchie around guarantees the smiles. It's one of the many gifts they bring. Yes, they're funny looking: the big eyes, big ears, squished nose, rows of wrinkles and lolling pink tongue are strange individual ingredients but put them together and they create a quirky whole that just makes you smile every time you set eyes on one. I'd be suspicious of anyone who looked at a Frenchie and didn't smile. There would be something wrong with someone like that, for sure.

I'm happy that I can say all this with the wisdom of hindsight because I remember when I had very little experience with dogs and all I wanted was – a dog. Simple as that. I just had the idea that a dog could bring that magical something that I needed in my life at that time, but I had no idea how much owning a dog would impact on my life in so many ways and where that huge feeling of responsibility for something other than myself would take me.

As you've read this far you will know by now that I didn't plan to take the Frenchie route; it was more that Frenchies found me. I had seen the little fellas around and thought they looked smart, but I had probably seen pugs and Boston terriers too and thought the same. It must have been the stand-out bat ears that did it for me in the end. I like how Frenchies wear them with pride and not embarrassment. They always hold their heads high with an air of defiance, as if to say: 'This is me, folks. If you don't like it, you know what you can do!' I admire that ballsy quality in the breed.

They're small, they look good and they have bags of personality which they want to heap on top of you. They want to be your dog so much that they smother you with love. There is so much more to a Frenchie than four legs and a would-be tail. Sometimes, with Ern, he had a self-assured look that seemed to be a dog version of two fingers up to anyone – or any dog – he didn't much care for. To my mind that kind of honesty is a massive part of the Frenchie's stack of special qualities – they don't give a toss for anyone who tries to bring them down (two legs or four) and for that they have my complete admiration.

Thinking about it, I'm sure this admiration for the gritty bit of the Frenchie personality comes from inside me. I'm sure any *TOWIE* viewer will have picked up by now that I get a lot of banter for my height and hair. It's OK … I can take it because I'm a big boy now and I've had years of the same comments, about my height anyway, and now it's pretty much water off a duck's back because I'm comfortable in my own skin. And I thank Ern for that because in many ways I am who I am because of Ern. He brought something out in me that I didn't know existed inside. He found a certain strength. It's not always been there, and bullies have had their day at my expense in the past. But like my nan always said … you have to stand up to bullies otherwise they win, and you can't afford to let that happen because they will take a part of you that you don't get back. Ever.

Perhaps I can relate to how Frenchies have suffered for their big ears and those wrinkles? So many people in the past wanted to breed those out – to take away the bits of them that made them different and some thought ugly. Being called the 'clown of the dog world' could be hurtful too, even though it's not meant to be. But, with a little help from their friends, the Frenchie has always squared up to the jibes and the agg with that big chest stuck out and head held high – and smiled. It's their way of handling bullies and I like it. Maybe I recognise a bit of me in there? Or at least I would like to.

I believe that some of that Frenchie magic has rubbed off on me – or, at least, I hope that it has. I feel stronger now than I did before Ern and to have such a mighty mate was bound to leave an impression on me. I don't want to get too close to giving dogs human qualities because I can see how dangerous that can be. Dogs are, after all, dogs and if we start to think of them as humans in fur coats we are in real trouble because a dog's needs are not the same as our own. But I've seen special qualities in Ern and Eric that I wish existed in many more human beings. You know what I mean?

Let's take those great, big Frenchie eyes for starters. If eyes really are the windows to the soul, then the Frenchie has a head start on all the other breeds combined. You can read stories about the legendary life-saving skills of the brandy-carrying St Bernards, the crazy speed of the greyhound and the super-sleuthing skills of the bloodhound but you look into the eyes of a Frenchie and you see their own version of extraordinary – a special friend.

Frenchies love to be loved. They crave affection from us as much as we need to feel the love from them. The first time I set eyes on Ernest he was with the rest of his litter but for me there was only one pup in that room. We connected and – please excuse me for being over-emotional here – it really was love at first sight. He looked at me and I looked at him and from that moment he was my dog. In those big black eyes of his I not only saw my future as a happy dog owner but I also felt the connection that I had hoped for. Something had clicked into place and when I took him home I knew that I was beginning a new phase in my life. I had a focus for my attention and my emotion. I wasn't lost or dead inside at all. Ern had arrived and I'm sure I sensed in him a vibe which said: 'Don't worry, Dad, we'll sort this together.' And I believed him.

What's really special is that he did sort me out. He made me open up and let in all the good emotions and let go of the bad stuff that I was allowing to eat away at me. Having Ern in my life made me a better person because, for a start, I had to think less of me and more about him. It was really only after I lost him that I gained a massive inner strength, drawing together all the energy, knowledge and, yes, anger, to take a fresh look at the wider world of Frenchies and start to put my thoughts into action. Ernest would have expected that of me. And I feel that he is watching to see what I do next for Frenchies and the world of dog welfare.

The way I see it, Frenchies are a dog for all people. For those who are looking for a small, compact and adaptable companion, these little geezers will fit right in. They don't need a lot of exercise: in fact, it's not healthy for them to take frequent or long walks. They like to be with you. To be honest they don't want to be anywhere else. They want to be as close to their owner as they can get – day and night and any other times in between if you can manage it.

But the downside, because there always seems to be a downside to something good, is their health. Frenchies are both blessed and cursed by their flat-faced features. Their big eyes capture your heart and that snuffling, snorting and snoring they do is part of their Frenchie charm. You always know when they are around because they are always making some kind of noise. Sadly, in reality, every breath they reach for and sometimes struggle through is a reminder that if you choose to invite one of these dogs into your life you are always going to be on health-watch. They can't be allowed to get over-excited or over-heated because if they do they could collapse in a panting heap – or even worse. You have to plan your days around this because, if you don't, the consequences could be dire. Believe me, I know.

Frenchies are vulnerable and it's sad and ironic that their popularity has made them even more vulnerable.

The greater the popularity of Frenchies, the more illegal breeding there is taking place to meet that demand. And now that I've been shown how cruel and uncaring the world of large-scale commercial puppy breeding and selling is – the world Eric came from – I can't just walk away. None of us should walk away. These lovely, loving, intelligent and knowing little dogs are not just an attractive accessory as I first thought – they are so very much more and in so many ways.

When I look into Eric's eyes I see love staring right back at me and I see a reflection of myself that is not the man I used to be before Ern. I now see someone who is less selfish and more understanding about dog ownership and who is more aware of the needs of all dogs, their invaluable friendship and their enduring capacity for love. That amount of affection and trust from a dog can sometimes be overwhelming and it can still take me aback. Not everyone allows themselves to open up to it and feel the benefit of it. I'm sure they have their reasons, but they are missing out on something special.

Being responsible for a dog is far more than just having a dog in the house. They love us – they need us. If I thought of them in any other way I would be betraying Eric and betraying Ern's memory.

I don't like confrontation – it never brings out the best

in me. It's not because I'm a coward, it's just that it rarely pays off and ends up with a lot of upset people who have shouted too loudly to hear anything that's said. Having said all of that, I won't shy away from givin' it large if I have to and to make my voice heard. If it involves my family, and in that I include Ern and Eric, I will fight to the death to defend them. That's why I admire people who crusade for the greater good of dogs and put some action behind their chat.

Ern and Eric have been my introduction to some incredible people and organisations who are fighting to raise the status of dogs in society. Eric was just looking for a home when I first met him at the centre, but giving him a home meant that I was introduced to the dark side of the trade in pedigree puppies and the people fighting for change. When I met Marc Abraham he was introduced to me as 'Marc the Vet' because that's how most people know him through his countless television appearances. I immediately realised that I had met a kindred spirit and this guy was serious about his campaign to improve legislation to ban third-party sales of pups and finally end the UK's cruel puppy farmimg industry, as well as removing the market for pups trafficked into the UK from abroad. Marc founded Pup Aid to make this happen so it was no surprise that we met at the House of Commons in the company of others who were standing up for animals. I've since discovered that Marc spends a lot of his time, when he's not treating animals at his practice near Brighton, in the company of MPs, battling for support on animal welfare issues. He uses his voice to make a difference and I admire that. That day at that event I knew that I had a place in this battle, not necessarily because of what I knew about puppy farms through having Eric, but because I knew I wanted to add my voice to the call out for better measures to protect animals. As I left that day I realised that I had found a kind of home with these kindred spirits and Ern had led me to the door.

Marc and those like him are the people who don't look the other way when there is a battle to fight on behalf of dogs in the world. They don't pretend they haven't seen it and carry on, blinkered to what's happening and what needs to be done to bring about change. This is the power of kindness.

I can lose my nut about things, but the power of kindness and understanding is the driving force behind change. Making others aware of issues that can be bettered with people power is more important to me now. Eric's arrival in my life was, without a shadow of a doubt, meant to be. The 'I'd like a dog' idea drove me to find Ernest, but it was the need to find Ern some companionship that led me to the rescue centre. Throw in the serendipity of the *TOWIE* team filming at my local centre in Essex and the rest, as they say, is history. But that was not the end of the story for me; it was more of a beginning.

When I saw Eric and his fellow smuggled pups my heart pounded – with anger. The puppy-smuggling trade and the conditions on puppy farms where breeding bitches are kept just about alive to supply the demand for pedigree pups in the UK – they disgust me. The more I heard, the angrier I became. I kept seeing Eric as a pup and imagining him in those terrible conditions, afraid and lost without his mum. There is no kindness or care in the trade and I can't bear to think of that going on, day in and day out, to innocent animals, including my beloved Frenchies. This very special breed has become a victim of its own success so thank goodness for the people who are fighting to secure legislation to stop this cruel trade in dogs. I support what they are doing with all my heart because I need to give something back to Frenchies and I do it in the name of the dogs who saved me.

Because without a shadow of a doubt, Ernest saved me.

That beautiful, handsome and brave Frenchie came into my life, turned it around, jiggled it up and generally set me on a new path to being happy. Some people say that it's good to retain your childhood innocence so that you welcome new experiences with the wide-eyed wonder of a little one rather than the cynical hardness of a grown-up. I'm good for that. I think if we expect something to be a certain way then the universe will deliver just that. I like to think of life always having the sparkle of excitement and the thrill of something new. Becoming a dog owner had all of that thrill and I believe that Ernest helped me to rediscover the child inside and the universe, in all its wonderful wisdom, delivered fun on four legs.

I loved Ernest instantly. I didn't expect that to happen at all – not with a dog. I honestly thought we would grow some mutual affection as we went along but fate had other plans. When I first met Ern I took him to my heart, but when the breeder told me he was already booked to go with someone else I knew that I had to stall the rush of emotion otherwise I was not going to be in a good place. Perhaps that's why, when the breeder called to say Ernest was mine if I wanted him, I went into happy overdrive – like a child on Christmas morning.

And that feeling didn't stop there.

When Ern first came home with me it was like being on an emotional rollercoaster with fear, joy, happiness, surprise, confusion, 'what the hell?' and 'are you taking the mickey, mate?' coming at me at high speed. For the first twenty-four hours – maybe thirty-six – it was chaos, and then the strangest and loveliest peace descended on us. Ern had arrived at just the right time to balance me out and pull all the strands of my life together. My job was changing and although I was considering something new I was not fully committed to the idea and felt as if I was in limbo with it all. The answers had to be out there somewhere but ... where?

One of the answers came in the shape of Ernest. The next came in the form of *TOWIE*. All change please! I was so lucky that Ern was made for television. Frenchies are respected for their adaptability and, if prizes were given out for being the best, Ern would have collected the gold star. He was my travel buddy, work buddy and photoshoot accessory. He did the lot and he loved it. I think there was something of the thespian or model in Ern because he loved the camera: I'm pretty sure he knew which was his best side. He always managed to wander round to the spot where the camera caught him at his best and, accidental or not, I admired him for that. Blimey, what a top dog! I couldn't have asked for a better companion to complement what I was doing at the time.

Naturally there were moments when having a dog who adores you is going to raise a few problems with other people from time to time and Ern's slobbering presence wasn't always appreciated or well timed. The boy had a habit of wanting to get too close at the wrong time and if I tell you that the question 'Does the dog have to be in the bedroom?' was always answered with the words 'Yes, I'm sorry, he does,' then I think you'll get the picture.

Ern was so much my dog that if we could have become physically attached just by spending all our waking and sleeping times together then we would have been a medical phenomenon. Remembering how I was sometimes in my life before Ern, I think he became my kind of other half. I don't mean we had some kind of weird partnership, just that he was almost the missing bit of me – the missing piece of my jigsaw puzzle at that time. With him around I was complete. In other words, I was not alone.

With Ern at my side I could walk into situations with him at my heel and we would handle things together. He was my wingman and I could look to him for a boost of confidence when it was needed. He never let me down and was always there for me. I didn't realise that this was how it would be to have a dog. If I had, I think I would have invited a dog into my life earlier. But then it wouldn't have been Ernest and maybe that's what it was all about. I was meant to have Ern and we were meant for each other. He needed to be loved and I needed the same.

I can't say that people were envious of me when it came

to Ern, but I think it's fair to say that people close to me were happy for me and others we met along the way thought it was very special and wished they had something like it. I guess it's like watching a couple in a restaurant who talk and laugh all evening with no awkward silences or need to fill gaps with meaningless small talk. Everyone envies those couples because it's rare for people to 'fit' so well. Dogs don't do awkward and they don't do small talk. The effortless comfort of life with dogs is one of the things that makes them so much more rewarding than people.

We were OK, me and Ern. We were muddling through together. It was like this dog had come into my life for a purpose. Just him being around helped me to rediscover a version of me that that existed before I began to screw things up. I know we all make mistakes, and there are things about ourselves that we can't bring ourselves to face because it's all too painful to relive. I was torturing myself going through my mistakes, but none of that mattered to Ern. Ern forgave me for all the things I didn't like about myself. It was as if having him around made me see things more clearly, and my responsibility to him helped me put things into perspective.

I'm not sure if I read it or made it up but I'm on the same track as the person who said: 'Making mistakes is better than faking perfection.' Ern understood all of that and I always knew that he had my back when the chips were down. My nan picked up on my sensitivity to dogs and reckoned that I connected with them better than I do with people and I've no doubt that she is right. My nan is always right and I'm sure could always see, especially with Ern, how we reflected each other's moods. I'm not putting myself out there as some kind of 'dog whisperer' or anything but there is some kind of connection with dogs ... something I know is there and only there when I'm in their company. I shared this with Ern right from the start and that's why there was no hiding his anxiety when his routine changed. We were sharing a home and life so there was no hiding place.

So when his normal routine started to shift about so that he was with me one minute and then Nan the next it started to upset and unsettle him, and I didn't like seeing my mate like that. The idea of getting a companion for Ern floated in and out of my head for a while and then I decided we would give it a try ... and, as you know, fate sorted the rest.

Enter stage left ... Eric, the little blue-fawn Frenchie with the troubled past. Had I taken too much on my hands this time? Ern needed a companion to put a stop to his separation anxiety and I needed to get this right – for all of us. With the addition of Eric, we were about to become a little family and life with my Wolfpack was about to take off.

If they considered me as 'dad' then Ern and Eric were 'brothers' and together we all helped each other in different ways. Ern was the stoic one for both of us. He was our guard and guardian who put us both on track. Eric is still the joker in the pack. He can't help it! His gift is the ability to make us laugh and wonder what he's going to get up to next. Eric is the doughnut in the family and I love him for it every day. Every time Eric acts the idiot when we're filming *TOWIE* I wonder if the camera crew will ever get tired of Eric getting in the way. They are so patient with him and understand that he doesn't seem to learn from his mistakes. Sometimes it feels similar to the chaos that can come from a 'take your child to work' day!'

I'm powerless to stop him turning every simple job into an 'event'. Just being around cameras, he can't help getting himself tangled up in the cables. There's always an untangling session that can turn a one-hour job into a three-hour one! There's no doubt about the fact that Eric runs rings around me in a way that Ernest never did, but it's lovely to see him enjoying himself with his friends on the set. That's worth its weight in gold.

And what did they both do for me? They kept me 'balanced', which was exactly what I needed at that time in my life. As the Wolfpack we were a solid unit sharing an unbreakable bond. My boys made me whole again and, in their own Frenchie way, gave me the confidence to feel that I had 'arrived' – I was sorted. I was me. And me was absolutely fine. Thank you very much.

Life was good. It felt like I had jumped on a carousel and everything was galloping along faster and faster and then suddenly someone put the brakes on and the whole thing crashed to a halt.

I don't think I had cried as an adult until I had Ernest but I know that I cried my heart out when I lost him. And without Ern in my universe, all the stars left my sky and smashed on the ground. I was in a very dark place and I think a small part of me still is.

It hit me hard when I realised that being the centre of someone's universe is a massive responsibility. I must have hit all the many stages of grief at various points, but I definitely let anger and guilt get the better of me. I didn't want to see anyone, and I didn't know what to say to the people who slipped through and tried to help me. I wanted to be alone, and I really meant that, because all I could do was cry. I couldn't speak about what had happened. It was too much to bear. If I spoke about it then it was real. If I stayed quietly away from everyone then maybe it wasn't true and I'd wake up from a terrifying sweat-drenched nightmare and the pain would be gone. It would all be over. Everything could go back to normal and the Wolfpack would be perfect again.

But the guilt kept a tight hold on me whatever sense I tried to make of it all. Not just a hatred for myself, for taking Ern and Eric out that day, but for bringing the dogs into my friends' and family's lives, sharing the love with them and then hitting them with the pain of loss too. Nan struggled with it so much. I gave her the two dogs to look after, and when I look back on it, I didn't give her much choice in the matter. That was something that really hit home when I lost Ern. She looked after them because she loves me and then she fell in love with the boys anyway – her other two 'grandsons', as she called them. So I put her in that position of having the dogs to love and then inflicted the grief and loss of Ern on her too. Guilt and grief had me running in circles. I never wanted to hurt my nan and that has left a very deep scar. I felt like I deserved the pain. She did not.

Looking back on those days in late August 2016 I really felt that life had handed me the fuzzy end of the lollipop. It had all been so good for a while and then, suddenly, the bottom fell out of my world. The unbelievable and long-lasting sadness of it all was that Ern was only three years old when I lost him. He was a happy lad but, as it turns out, he didn't have good health on his side. I kept asking myself – was I such a bad dad? What did I do – or not do – for Ern that took him from us so soon?

The vet told me that I couldn't have known but I still feel bad about it. Now I know more about the breed and how vulnerable their popularity has made them I don't just feel sad about Ern's death, I feel angry … and partly responsible. I remember lying with him on the bathroom floor that terrible day, just wanting to take his pain away. But I couldn't. And that feeling still kills. I know it always will.

To be honest, I am haunted by Ern's final moments.

Even though I don't believe that time heals all wounds, since losing the lad and having time to think everything through a million times over, I have found one glimmer of hope: I can see now how something good can come out of such sadness. After Ernest died and life settled into what it had to be – Eric, home, family, work and friends and all that comes with it   I think the loss triggered a kind of reset button inside me. Grief is one thing but sitting around contemplating my naval wasn't going to get me anywhere or help Eric, was it? I'm sure that if Ern could have sent me a message, he would have been the one with his paw on that reset button saying, in his best Ray

Winstonesque tones: 'Come on, mate!' I want to imagine that Eric would have followed up with a good rasp of chatty Alan Carr: 'Yeah right, and let's have some fun along the way!'

Grief is a very powerful emotion. If it can be harnessed I believe great things can be achieved and, for me, that means positive action to help Frenchies and any breed of dog that is being, hurt, abused or mistreated by humans. There is so much that can be done to reach out to other people who love Frenchies and love all dogs as much as I do. So here we are. From the start of my journey to the end … wanting a dog, loving that dog, losing that dog and now making use of the grief in a positive way.

I don't think I will get any peace of mind until I have played my part in this. This, for me, is Ern's legacy. You see, I couldn't help him, I couldn't save him when he needed me most, but I *can* help others in his memory. So that's what I will do. That way the Wolfpack lives on.

In December 2017, I was very privileged to see the kindness of others when I witnessed the work of Humane Society International (HSI) in South Korea, where the charity is working tirelessly to close down dog meat farms and to educate and compensate the farmers who have come to rely on this cruel trade for their livelihood. I joined them on a mission to rescue 170 dogs from a farm where they were being kept in deplorable conditions. I truly believe that in some way Ern gave me the inner strength I needed to go on this journey. It's something I had wanted to do for a very long time but I needed to know that I would be able to face the horrors that exist on these farms and still be hands-on helpful to the charity's rescue team while I was there. That was important to me.

I forced myself to watch footage captured by the HSI team showing the cruel reality of the dog meat trade because I wanted to know as much as I could before I went out there but, to be honest, nothing could have prepared me for what I witnessed. Being there with the dogs on death row is like being in a living nightmare. It was far, far worse than I ever imagined.

All you can see is row upon row of cages where the breeding dogs and puppies are kept ready for the meat markets. It was absolutely heartbreaking to see them. Even more heartbreaking was that the dogs greeted us with no fear and looked like they wanted to be cuddled. I was desperate to take them all home but had to be satisfied with the news that out of the 170 dogs we rescued on that mission, 157 were destined for rehabilitation and rehoming centres in the US and Canada and a lucky thirteen were coming to the UK. One of the dogs I handled during the operation was a leggy black pup that the team called Adam. This lad looked like a Labrador but with a streak of Korean Jindo thrown in, and when I first saw him he was staring at me through the bars of a cage where he had probably lived most of his life. Adam was on death row, and knowing the dogs go to the meat market at around twelve months old, this little guy was very close to being slaughtered and eaten.

Adam was caked in mud and his own dirt and got very jumpy when we went to open his cage. The poor dog probably wondered what we were going to do to him. I'd seen the footage of the farmers yanking the dogs from their cages when it was their time to die and Adam would have seen that happen lots of times. There's no guessing what would have happened to him and the others if we hadn't turned up when we did.

The thing with Adam was, unlike some of the other dogs, he still had a spark in his eye. He had his tail between his legs, but he wanted to get out of that cage and I just couldn't leave his story there. Even though I knew he was now safe I wanted to be at the airport to see him and welcome all the dogs when they landed at London Heathrow on 4 January 2018.

It was amazing to see the plane land, knowing the lucky thirteen, including Adam, were on board and heading for their new lives in the UK. It breaks my heart every time I think about what would have happened to them if HSI had not intervened. And this was only one of the charity's many valuable rescues and there's so much more to do. I am committed to helping them more in any way I can.

Just seeing the dogs' crates being lifted off the plane was a great moment because although the little guys didn't know it, they would be OK now. They were still dirty, and some were understandably traumatised, so much so that they wouldn't leave their crates right away because they were just too afraid. But for the others who did take their first steps on UK soil it was amazing.

Remember, they had only lived in cages, so they had never seen, smelt or put their paws on grass before. It was funny and fabulous to watch them take in this incredible new experience called 'going for a walk on a lead' and high-stepping along as if they were wearing moon boots! And Adam? Well I couldn't wait to see him safe in the UK so opening the door of his crate at Heathrow was the best moment of the day.

He was a bit skittish and was still holding his tail between his legs, but he was one of four dogs – Adam, Abby, Mocha and Jack – who were able to face the cameras and go on their first walk with us. Jack the beagle was scenting and tracking right away. He was just being a beagle and it was a beautiful sight. I cried a lot that morning but this time all the tears were to do with the relief and happiness. This was the flip-side of crying when I saw the same dogs suffering on the meat farm in South Korea. This was pure magic.

I said to each one of those dogs that day at the airport: 'You'll be alright now mate. You're in safe hands and you'll have a new and happy life here like you will only have ever dreamt of before.' I had already decided to keep a special eye on Adam, who had gone from being a nervous but friendly dog, to a dog with bright eyes looking for cuddles and wagging his tail. It was like he was celebrating being alive and he wanted me to join in the celebration! When my mates from HSI said that I could take Adam home that night and do a bit of foster care I leapt at the chance. Eric was already staying with Mum and Nan, so I didn't have to worry about him. I knew it wouldn't be fair to introduce the dogs to each other as it could be too much for both of them. Besides, he was going to need plenty of one-to-one attention to build his confidence in people and I wasn't in a position to be all of that for him. But I could be his companion for the first few hours of his new life.

He was as good as gold in the car and, although he wasn't sure about the feel of the wooden floor, the rugs or the idea of sitting on a sofa, he loved taking his first bath! Water coming out of the showerhead foxed him a bit. He kept looking at me, then the stream of water, then back at me as he splashed around all wet and soapy. By the time his bath was over we were both soaked to the skin, and then came the fun of drying him with a towel and rolling him around on the floor playing. While I was doing all this, I couldn't help reminding myself that this beautiful dog could have ended up on someone's plate. That killed me.

I slept on the sofa with him that night and he woke me up at 3am licking my face. He wanted to go for a wee, so I let him out and he came back in, settled back down on me, and fell fast asleep. How normal is that? What an amazing dog! He didn't make any mess in the house – other than scooting over a coffee table and knocking over a cup of tea. Not bad for a dog that had lived his life in a cage. I was in awe of this dog and the next day, when we appeared on *Good Morning Britain*, he faced the lights, camera, action of a television studio like a true pro! He let me brush him and fix his barnet before we went on the sofa and stuck close to me the whole time, showing what a terrific and loving dog he is. He probably thought he was living a doggy dream or something, but Adam is a dog needing a second chance. He needs lots of attention and exercise and a comfy home and more than anything he craves love.

I'll be keeping an eye on this guy. I vowed that day to follow his story and maybe I will be able to become part of Adam's new life in some way.

Second chances. It's all about a second chance at life when everything looks so hopeless. At every turn I couldn't help imagining Eric in one of the cages and imagined how powerless I would be trying to get him home. Most of the dogs that are not already there as breeding dogs are pets that have been caught and rounded up to be eaten. It's so alien to our culture and to us it is barbaric. And when you see very familiar breeds such as golden retrievers, spaniels and beagles in the cages it messes with your head so much. I cried. I knew that I would. How could anyone not cry when you are presented with such horror? HSI will always have my support until the dog meat trade is banned. I have promised Ern and Eric that I will do all I can to help on their behalf. And that is just the start.

For as long as I carry my love for Ern in my heart I will always be looking to honour his memory. I know that he would be telling me to stand up for my beliefs and that's what I intend to do. I know that he would want me to put my voice to highlighting the underworld of puppy smuggling to help others in the same situation as Eric. Like the dog meat farms, it's another cruel industry where money, not love, is the main drive. They prey on the popularity of the Frenchie and the ignorance of the people who just want to get their hands on one of these perfect little dogs.

Turning grief into action is much better and much healthier than talking about it and doing absolutely nothing. We should all look for a passion to follow, a campaign to lend our names to and a path to make a difference. We all have a voice – we just need to use it.

Memories can drive us on to do great things: things we perhaps never thought we were capable of. I have many pictures of Ern around my flat, so he still looks at me with those big beautiful eyes and I can still talk to him. I think he would like that. A large black and white image of me with the dogs dominates one wall. It was a gift and I will never remove it. Having that image there means that Ern is still with us every day. I still have his ashes because I haven't found the heart or the courage to scatter them yet – maybe I never will. It is such a personal thing, but only I know when the time is right to let him go.

I know that people who have not lost a pet don't really understand how the loss can hit so hard but I can assure you there is nothing like this pain. It's hard to put into words but some manage it better than others and when I saw actor Tom Hardy's eulogy to his dog Woody recently, I could have cried with the guy. People who have a connection with their pets can feel the loss as keenly as losing a person that's close to them. For people who have no one but the pet then they are losing their only friend, their only companion – their partner, their everything. Losing a pet can be very debilitating, leaving folk unable to go to work, look after themselves or function normally. Grief can't be underestimated, and it's different for everyone so it should never be brushed away or laughed at. And some people do react like that because I'm sorry to say they simply don't understand.

Losing Ern really cracked open my sensitive soul and the images that I would rather forget of his last hours on this earth play in my head like a horror movie – if I let them. The secret is not to let them. I know, easier said than done. But I still have Eric to think of, so it is easier for me in so many ways. After Ern's death I had Eric looking at me, those big sadder than normal eyes asking me what was I going to do next. I couldn't do anything much for a while. But he stuck with me and then I knew that whatever I did do next it had to be for him. We were in this as a team. This was the start of Life After Ern and it was up to us to sort it out together.

I think me and Eric are growing up together and what Ern didn't manage to fit in teaching me before he was called away to a higher place, Eric will teach me as we go along. And we'll have some fun along the road too. Eric will see to that.

There are some practical reminders too: Eric still hates getting into the back of the car. He was always happy to be there sitting alongside Ern, taking in the air of the open window and watching the world go by with his brother and best mate beside him. But now he will only sit on the front seat. He has a harness so I can be sure he's safe but he won't go anywhere near the spot where Ern lay on his last trip in the car. He just can't do it and gets very distressed no matter what I try. It adds to the guilt that I can't help him. That I can't take his pain away – because if I could, I would in a heartbeat.

I'm sure that losing Ern has made me more protective of Eric and I don't take anything for granted where he is concerned. For instance, when I'm out having a drink with friends I always make sure that we're in a shady spot for Eric and that he has a bowl of water right beside him. I can't leave it up to him to put himself in the shade, I just need to make sure he's safe.

Sometimes when I have Eric along I prepare myself for a long day. I know it makes it more of an expedition than a day trip, but I want to make travelling as stress-free as possible for him. We split tube journeys and take taxis (although it can be tough to find a taxi that will take a dog) and wait for later, quieter trains if it helps him.

I remember having to take him into London for a meeting last year when it took us four hours to get home, mixing trains and taxis, with a wait around in a rain shower to cool off. Eric was very cool alright, and he was calm and collected when we got home. He just wanted his supper and then he took himself off to bed! I was pretty much frazzled after the day's events and Eric was probably wondering what I was puffing and panting about but it was worth the longer day. Eric was relaxed and happy. It was me who needed to take a chill-pill!

The way I look at it is, this is only what a parent would do for a small child. And when we travel together, I build in extra time because I know our journey will take longer with lots of rest times for Eric. If we're on a train or walking to meetings, anything like that, I like to let people know that we're moving at Eric's pace. It's not a problem. I plan all of this into our days and it's how it is and how it has to be for his sake. If Eric's safe and happy – then all is right with my world.

Ern and Eric weren't blood brothers, but they were brothers in every other way. And what a bloody fabulous big brother Ern was. When I took Ern to the rescue centre to meet Eric for the first time I was praying that Ern would like the little blue guy that I had already fallen for. But as I've told you, if he hadn't taken to Eric the way I had and we had walked away that day leaving him behind, I would still have gone back to visit him. I would have camped outside the centre until I had seen Eric on his way to his forever home. If I couldn't be his person then I wanted to congratulate the people who were going to be lucky enough to share their life with him. I could already tell he was going to be a special kind of guy. I just knew that he would make up our little family. And this time I knew that I was up to the job.

Of course I was lucky that Ern thought Eric was the bee's knees too! But who couldn't love him? Blue-fawn, solid, tank-like, smooth and wrinkled all at the same time. Velvety body with a suede nose, soft feet, big ears, bustling and busy, into everything, swaying, jogging and all with the sound of a small engine. And together? What a pair plodding along together, Ern slightly ahead and Eric happy to follow. The big lad and the soft lad ... my lads. The Wolfpack.

For now, every time I look at Ern in a photograph or when I come across an old episode of *TOWIE*, I smile at the sight of my faithful shadow and I'm reminded that he left me with a purpose. I could try to rationalise it all and say that maybe Ern was here with me for a season or a reason rather than a lifetime. I didn't get the lifetime, the ten to fourteen years that I was looking forward to, so maybe he came for a reason to teach me about myself. Maybe he was in my life to lead me down avenues where I could see I needed to go, and to teach me how being less selfish could go a long way. Losing Ern has rebooted me, in a good way. This new journey will be with him at my side, I know I will feel him there nudging his body next to mine. I'm even thinking about dedicating a new tattoo to Ern. I have thought about it often, and I still have some space for him, but it must be right. My feelings for Ern are more than skin deep but to have him with me in such a visual way is ... almost inevitable.

Ern taught me a lot about myself when he was alive, but his loss taught me more.

His kindness taught me that a dog's love is the most honest emotion any human being will ever experience. A dog doesn't know any other way. What you see is what you get. That's one of the things that makes sharing your life with a dog so great. They don't judge you. To them, you're great just the way you are.

They don't shed a whisker if you haven't showered for

days, and they don't have a meltdown at the sight of your new rubbish tattoo, or keep reminding you that the top belongs on the toothpaste. A dog craves your attention, your time and your care. Ern was a party boy, like me: he loved to play, he liked being groomed and loved his grub. We were mates who muddled through the rest together. I learnt from Ern that dogs who are loved, well socialised and fed a balanced diet are not only healthy but happy too. It's not a lot to ask of us owners really, is it? Just to be thoughtful, responsible and never cruel. If we can manage to do this, a dog will be a best friend for life and, believe me, as a bloke with a lasting love for two Frenchies ... life doesn't get sweeter.

Thank you, Ern. Long live the Wolfpack.

Acknowledgements

Thank you to ...

My Nan ... for always being you, and for being best friend to Ernest and Eric and treating them better that you treat me!

My Mum ... for putting up with me and all my crazy ideas!

Wendy Higgins and everyone in the team at Humane Society International (HSI) UK ... for your courageous work and for inviting me to join their rescue operation in South Korea.

The great TOWIE team ... you know who you are!

Lorna Russell and Lucy Oates at Virgin Books ... for your massive support with this book and believing in me at every step.

Marc Abraham ... for your support and invaluable veterinary advice.

Gemma Wheatley, Nadia King and the team at Mokkingbird ... for making this happen.

James Rudland ... for being an excellent photographer and an all-round good geezer.

Lauren Dickinson ... for being there for me.

Izzy George ... for your friendship and for helping me tell my story.